—"is he at all like you?"— I must say —No— ...
personal appearance — he being stout — & goodlooking...
(speaking botanically,) that is —lanky —& considerably ugly,— ... as ... you
... I can judge — very — opposite.— I believe I am any thing but candid: in
fact — I am naturally suspicious — & exceedingly reserved: the first good
quality arises from my having seen plenty of the Evil part of the world from
my youth up — the second from being but very little used to company or society.
... for excepting Mr. Yarrell — (whom Mr. Hewitson & Mr. Atkinson know,) ... to whom I
go to study bones & muscles — I don't know a single person in all London
to visit intimately. This is very odd, but no less true.— As for taking any
of your lively, writing amiss — I should be a very great goose to do so: ... little
... contrary — I laugh sometimes by whatever other — & always read them with
a vast gusto. — Do you know a Mr. Sharpe of Bamborough Castle?
I was introduced to him some time back —& he asked me to come
there: I should not wonder if I see Northumberland — before you
... in town: — I am ... rather ... interested in the North, &
'tis ... I should have ... he procured so many subscribers
... originaly — my ... mother's family were ...
from Durham — although ... I am so little of
a genealogist that — ... Jarnysyde & Brignall
... all I can recollect of the names —& Sunnisice
... their residence. Pray is there such a place in being now? ...
At the corner of the paper I shall insert a very accurate
portrait of myself — thinking it highly proper you should have
some idea of what sort of a being your correspondent is, &
begging — if you are at all inclined to be wrathful at my levity
to remember that I am only 19 years old —& am only as merry
as I am now about once in 6 weeks.— You will be pleased to
hear I am engaged in a Zoological Work, shortly to appear from that
society — also in a work on Tortoises by a very celebrated
Zoologist Thomas Bell —& a very kind friend to me. I will
send you an India Proof shortly — though 'tis not much
in your way. — Now — you will think me very stupid;
but when I sent last — I packed up 8 & ... number 7 —
promising to send the 3 extra sets — (which I am about to do —) thus
making up for 11 subscribers.— Did I by accident
enclose 11 of number 7 for you? (not including the Brandling...)

N.B. this is amazingly like; add only — that both my knees are fractured from being run over,
which has made them very peculiarly crooked — that my neck is singularly long —
& a most elephantine nose — & a disposition to tumble here & there — owing to being halfblind,
and you may very well imagine my fout ensemble.

JOHN LEHMANN

# EDWARD LEAR
## and his world

*with 137 illustrations*

THAMES AND HUDSON

*On half-title page:* Letter from Edward Lear to C. Empson, dated 1 October 1831, with a sketch of himself: '. . . I am only 19 years old – and am only as merry as I am now about once in 6 weeks. – You will be pleased to hear I am engaged in a Zoological Work, shortly to appear . . . – also on a work on Tortoises. . . .' Referring to the self-portrait at the bottom right of the letter, Lear added: '. . . this is amazingly like; add only – that both my knees are fractured from being run over, which has made them very peculiarly crooked – that my neck is singularly long, – a most elephantine nose – and a disposition to tumble here and there – owing to being half blind. . . .'

*Frontispiece:* Black and red chalk drawing of Edward Lear by W. Holman Hunt, 7 November 1857.

*Opposite:* Sketch of Lear at the Royal Academy Schools, from a letter written by him to Chichester Fortescue in January 1850.

Printed in Great Britain by Jarrold and Sons Ltd, Norwich

EDWARD LEAR   *Left by his friend to breakfast alone on the white*
*Italian shore, his Terrible Demon arose*
*Over his shoulder; he wept to himself in the night,*
*A dirty landscape-painter who hated his nose.*

*The legions of cruel inquisitive They*
*Were so many and big like dogs: he was upset*
*By Germans and boats; affection was miles away:*
*But guided by tears he successfully reached his Regret.*

*How prodigious the welcome was. Flowers took his hat*
*And bore him off to introduce him to the Tongs;*
*The demon's false nose made the table laugh; a cat*
*Soon had him waltzing madly, let him squeeze her hand;*
*Words pushed him to the piano to sing comic songs;*

*And children swarmed to him like settlers. He became a land.*

*W. H. Auden*
*January 1939*

ONE DAY IN 1832 LORD STANLEY, heir to the twelfth Earl of Derby, stood watching a young man of twenty making drawings of the animals in the London Zoological Gardens in Regent's Park. Lord Stanley was a keen naturalist, and had devoted part of his great wealth to creating an unique private menagerie at the family estate of Knowsley Hall, near Liverpool. He had for some time been looking for an artist who could help him in his plan to publish an illustrated book on his rare collection. He had consulted Dr Gray of the British Museum, and Dr Gray had mentioned a remarkable young draughts-man who had already achieved a considerable reputation with his *Illustrations of the Family of Psittacidae.* This book consisted of forty-two coloured lithographs of parrots, the first folio publication of its kind to be produced in England by an English artist, and still thought to be one of the finest, most accurate, most sensitive, most brilliantly realized illustrated works of natural history ever published. The plates in it were judged by some contemporary connoisseurs to be the equal of the famous bird studies by Barraband and Audubon. Lord Stanley was evidently deeply impressed by what he saw of the young artist at work, introduced himself and asked him to come and live at Knowsley and make drawings of the menagerie.

The young man jumped at the offer, and spent the next four years in the Earl of Derby's household. His name was Edward Lear. He was tall, with a slight stoop, no doubt caused partly by having to peer very closely through his strong spectacles at whatever he was drawing, and also by his extremely delicate health. He was not in any way good-looking, but his sensitively pleasing expression and the humorous twinkle in his eye made up for a general plainness and the large, shapeless nose of which he was painfully conscious all his life.

The years at Knowsley were a turning-point in Lear's life. They gave him not only a livelihood and a patron, but the chance of be-coming known to other patrons in the aristocratic circles in which Lord Derby and his family moved. They also gave him the oppor-tunity of developing other gifts which he discovered in himself, in particular for the entertainment of children by the writing and illustrating of nonsense poetry. In the course of time he acquired the

7

Knowsley Hall, seat of the Earls of Derby, from a nineteenth-century engraving.

Edward, thirteenth Earl of Derby, who as Lord Stanley had invited Lear to the family seat at Knowsley in 1833: watercolour by William Derby, 1837.

reputation of being the supreme poet of nonsense, though his supremacy was challenged twenty years after the publication of his first book of limericks by the rather different genius of Lewis Carroll. The nonsense books brought him not only fame but money, though never enough for him to give up the career he chose for himself as a landscape painter. The output of drawings and watercolours which he produced on his travels was immense, and since his death the regard in which they are held has steadily grown – though his elaborate oil paintings, in sharp contrast, have to a large extent lost their appeal. The Journals he wrote during those travels are also now highly esteemed for their immense readability, their freshness of observation and their humour. He is, in fact, seen at last as a many-sided genius, one of the most original of the Victorian age. He was also a most lovable human being, loyal, affectionate, selfless in his dealings with his many friends, an enchanter of children and a source of constant mirth that forever bubbled out of a temperament that, in its secret depths, was never free of melancholy for long.

*Opposite:* A page from Lear's sketchbook, probably done between 1830 and 1835 when he was drawing at the Zoological Gardens, with pencil drawings of birds, feathers, animals, and landscapes.

*Above left:* A drawing of Lear's mother Ann.

*Above right:* Bowman's Lodge, Holloway, home of the Lear family in Edward's childhood: nineteenth-century engraving.

Edward Lear was born in Holloway on 12 May 1812 (the same year as Charles Dickens and Robert Browning). His father, Jeremiah, was a stockbroker and also engaged in sugar-refining, a business in which his family had been active since the middle of the eighteenth century. In 1788 he married Ann Clark Skerrett, and went to live with her in Pentonville. They had a very large family, of which Edward was the twentieth child; many of his brothers and sisters died as babies, as was so often the case in those days. Edward Lear himself in later years maintained that his grandfather was of Danish stock and originally spelt his name LØR, but whether he actually believed this story or not, it was certainly untrue. Perhaps he had his tongue in his cheek when he told people this rather romantic-sounding fiction: it has a slight touch of the nonsense-writer about it.

What is true is that by the time he was born the family had moved to a simple but elegant house of Georgian design, Bowman's Lodge, in the still unspoilt village of Holloway. The air was healthy, and the house, standing high up above London, had an impressive view south towards the smoke-hazed city below it. Lear was in the habit of maintaining that he could remember 'every particle' of his life from a very early age. One of his most vivid memories was of being wrapped in a blanket one night and taken to a window to see the illuminations that celebrated the victory of Waterloo.

Soon after that, in 1816, his father met with financial disaster, and the family had to leave Bowman's Lodge, though it appears that they eventually returned to it when Jeremiah managed to pull himself out of debt. But the days of comparative affluence were over, and Edward's mother had an extremely difficult time coping with her large brood. The little boy was entrusted to his eldest sister Ann, who had the good fortune to have been left a small private income of £300 a year by her grandmother. From that time on she acted as his mother; she was twenty-one years older, and her loving, deeply understanding care of him continued all her life. Lear once wrote of her: 'She has always been as near to Heaven as it is possible to be.' And when she died in 1861 he was heartbroken. He told a friend: 'I am all at sea and do not know my way an hour ahead. I shall be so terribly alone.'

What would have happened to Lear if he had not had Ann's unfailing devotion, it is difficult to imagine. He was an extremely delicate boy, suffering from frequent attacks of bronchitis and asthma, and, more seriously, from the age of six or seven, from fits of epilepsy. It seems likely that this was the less violent form known as the *petit mal*; but the fits were frequent, often as many as eighteen in a month, and caused him constant worry and distress. They made him hyper-sensitive and shy in the presence of strangers, and were probably one of the chief reasons for his long periods of depression, which he referred to as 'the Morbids'. He never alluded to his epilepsy in his letters, but in his private diaries he called it 'the Demon' or 'the Terrible Demon'.

Ann Lear, Edward's sister, who brought him up.

Obviously a frail boy of such uncertain health was not cut out for the rough-and-tumble of an early nineteenth-century boarding school. Though he referred now and then in later life to having gone to school at the age of eleven, nothing is known of this episode and it seems likely that it did not last long. Almost all his education came from Ann, and from his own browsings among the books he found at home. He discovered the modern poets, fell in love with Byron, studied books of natural history with avidity, and acquired a deep love of painting. His father appears to have had a good collection of pictures, and to have encouraged his children to appreciate them, and to draw and paint themselves. One of the downstairs rooms in Bowman's Lodge, across from the nursery, was set aside as the 'painting room', and became the boy's favourite haunt.

From the age of eleven or twelve, Edward made frequent visits to his married sister Sarah's home at Arundel. He came to love the peaceful landscape of the Sussex downs, made a number of new friends among the neighbouring families, and learned that, even at that early age, he had a natural talent for making people laugh – affectionately – at his whimsical observations and oddities of behaviour. For his future development as an artist, the most important event of those Sussex visits was probably making the acquaintance of the Earl of Egremont, whose stately home at Petworth, twelve miles to the north of Arundel, was filled with the works of famous painters of the day. There is little doubt that Lear's passionate admiration for Turner, and the dawn of his ambition to become a landscape painter himself, date from this period.

The Zoological Gardens, Regent's Park, in 1835.

*Opposite:* 'Pan Troglodytes – Chimpanzee with clothes on', watercolour and pencil, drawn by Lear while at Knowsley.

In any case, before he had reached the age of sixteen, he had decided to try and earn a living by drawing and painting. He and Ann moved into a top-floor flat off the Gray's Inn Road, and there he began, in the humblest fashion, to make sketches to sell in the shops for a few shillings, to colour prints and paint fans and screens; and, more unusually, to make what he described as 'morbid disease drawings, for hospitals and certain doctors of physic'. Very soon, however, he developed a particular interest in the preparation of pictures of birds for the lavishly illustrated ornithological and zoological books that were coming into vogue at that time. He worked at first with a well-known naturalist, Prideaux Selby, and appears to have gained confidence so rapidly that by 1830 he had decided to tackle a book on his own. As I have already described, he chose the parrot family as his special province, and obtained permission to make drawings from the live specimens in the recently opened Zoological Gardens. He used a lithographic process rather than wood-engraving, the more usual process of the period, and when he was satisfied with the plates, generally had the prints coloured by someone else to his exact specifications. This was an extremely bold project for so young an artist, but not beyond his powers, as the connoisseurs quickly recognized when the first two folios of the fourteen he originally planned were published in a strictly limited edition.

He worked very hard all through 1830 and 1831, and was finding the strain severe and the costs heavy. He decided to give up after he had finished twelve folios, but his reputation as a zoological draughtsman was made. He then turned to other creatures in the zoo, including tortoises, terrapins and turtles. It was while he was at work on these that the great stroke of luck occurred of the invitation to Knowsley.

*Opposite:* Salmon-crested cockatoo, from *Illustrations of the Family of Psittacidae,* Lear's first work as an ornithological draughtsman, which was published in folios between 1830 and 1832.

*Right:* T. H. Maguire's portrait of Prideaux Selby, the author (with Sir William Jardine) of *Illustrations of British Ornithology.* Lear worked with him between 1828 and 1830.

*Below:* Lelerang or Javan squirrel, from *Gleanings from the Menagerie at Knowsley Hall,* privately printed in 1846, which contained reproductions of some of Lear's drawings done at Knowsley.

*Above:* Blue and yellow macaw, one of the first published engravings by Lear, from *The Gardens and Menagerie of the Zoological Society Delineated,* 1931.

There was a sick man of Tobago
Liv'd long on rice-gruel and sago;
   But at last, to his bliss,
   The physician said this—
"To a roast leg of mutton you
   may go."

The first known limerick, by an
unknown author, from *Anecdotes and
Adventures of Fifteen Gentlemen*
(*c.* 1822).

Portrait of John Gould by T.H.
Maguire, 1849. Gould was a
naturalist, author of *The Birds of
Europe* and many other volumes, for
whom Lear worked as an illustrator
in the early 1830s with very little
acknowledgment.

Lord Stanley's father, the genial and gregarious Earl of Derby, was nearly eighty years old but still enjoyed being the head of an enormous establishment, where friends and relations were always welcome. Anything between forty and one hundred guests, children, grandchildren and great-grandchildren would sit down to dinner. Lear himself was treated at the beginning as one of the staff, and ate below stairs with the upper servants. It was not long, however, before the old man noticed that the younger members of the household were taking to excusing themselves as soon as they could, and disappearing. He then discovered that their destination was the steward's room, where the young artist who had so recently arrived would entertain them with comic drawings and absurd rhymes. Hearing this, the Earl immediately invited Lear to join him and the rest of the household for dinner upstairs, where he soon overcame his shyness and won the affection of the whole family.

One day one of the guests (or so one conjectures), delighted by his inventions, brought to his attention a book, published about 1822, called *Anecdotes and Adventures of Fifteen Gentlemen*. It had amusing illustrations to a text consisting of verses cast in a form that has come to be known as the limerick, no one is quite sure why. One of them ran as follows:

> There was a sick man of Tobago
> Liv'd long on rice-gruel and sago;
>    But at last, to his bliss,
>    The physician said this—
> 'To a roast leg of mutton you may go.'

It seems that Lear immediately saw that this was an ideal form in which to exploit his gift for comic invention in rhyme and drawing. He began forthwith to invent limericks for the Stanley grandchildren. They were a great success, and not only with this youngest audience. In 1846, more than twelve years later, he published his first collection of these limericks: he called it *A Book of Nonsense*, but he did not reveal himself as the author, taking instead the *nom de plume* of 'Derry down Derry'.

Meanwhile, the climate of Lancashire was beginning to tell on him. He did not spend the whole of the years between 1832 and 1836 at Knowsley, but went back to London from time to time, to be with Ann and to go on with the illustrative work with which he had agreed to help the well-known zoologist John Gould, who had little talent as an artist. He enrolled at a school of art in Bloomsbury, but does not appear to have stayed there very long. In the summer of 1835 he went on a trip to Ireland, and walked through the Wicklow Mountains with Arthur Stanley, who belonged to another branch

*Umbrellifera*, Kendal, 1836. Lear
made a tour of the Lake District in
the summer of that year.

of the Stanley family. The following summer he visited the Lake District. From both trips he brought back a sheaf of drawings: his eyesight was getting too strained to work any longer on the minute detail of the bird illustrations, and it seems that the pleasure he had in making these landscape drawings, and the admiration with which they were received, decided him finally to make a career of them. At the same time his health had deteriorated to the point where he realized that he must go abroad to find a milder climate. Lord Stanley, who had now become the thirteenth Earl, was quick to sympathize, and with his nephew Robert Hornby provided Lear with the means to go to Rome, where he would be able to continue his studies in painting and, as they hoped, recuperate. He set off in July 1837, lingered much on the way, in Bavaria, Milan and Florence in particular, and did not reach Rome until November. He had a bursting portfolio of sketches with him, and his hopes were high.

*Overleaf: page 18*, St Peter's, Rome,
from Arco Oscuro, watercolour,
1840; *page 19*, stairs leading to S.
Pietro in Vincoli, Rome,
watercolour, 1838.

Ar. Oscuri.
march 4. 1840 —

Roma 17 7br 1838

Pen and ink drawing for *Robinson Crusoe* by Thomas Stothard. Lear's enthusiasm for landscape was at least partly inspired by the 'beautiful Stothard drawings, those exquisite creations of landscape which first made me, when a child, long to see similar realities' (see also pp. 87, 90).

From this time until his old age Lear became a wanderer, never settling long in any one place, though for the first few years after his departure from England he made Rome, filled as it was at that time with artists and patrons of artists, his main base. He made frequent excursions all over the Mediterranean lands and even further east, and only returned to England for brief periods, except during the years between 1849 and 1853, when he became a student in London at the Schools of the Royal Academy. This was partly because he had a restless temperament and an insatiable appetite for new travel experiences, but also, of course, because he needed constant new material for the drawings and paintings out of which he was making his livelihood. He explored Italy south of Rome; he went on a long expedition in 1847 to Calabria, Sicily and the Kingdom of Naples, which is recorded in the second published volume of *Journals of a Landscape Painter*; in the following two years he visited the Ionian Islands, then under British suzerainty, and travelled all over Greece and Albania, as described in his *Journals of a Landscape Painter in Albania and Illyria*, which were in fact published before the Italian Journals. After 1854, for much of the next four years, he was in Corfu, as industrious as ever; in fact one may almost say that Corfu became his special province as a painter, for he revisited it on several subsequent occasions between 1861 and 1866. During this period he also visited Egypt and the Holy Land, and penetrated as far as Petra. In 1868 he made a spring excursion to Corsica, which produced the last of his published Journals in 1870.

By this time he had begun to think that he should live a more settled and less roving life, tried Cannes at first and then, a few years later, moved to San Remo, where he bought a plot of land and built a home which he called the Villa Emily. This was a very happy period in his life. He spent his time painting, entertaining a constant stream of visitors who wanted to see his work (but far too seldom bought), composing more nonsense songs, and gardening. At first he said: 'Tho' I like flowers and a garden, I don't like working in it.' Soon, however, the fascination grew, and he passed long hours in his garden, finding 'the picking off of caterpillars and the tying up of creepers no end of distraction'. Nevertheless, in spite of the fact that

he had grown fat and highly sensitive to the discomforts of travel, his restlessness had not been altogether quelled. In 1872, at the age of sixty, he was invited to India and decided to set out on the long-dreamed-of voyage. He turned back at Suez owing to difficulties of transport, but was off again the next year, and spent more than twelve months indomitably travelling all over the sub-continent and the island of Ceylon as well. In the end, however, the vastly ambitious enterprise became too much for him, and he returned to San Remo exhausted and in far from good health.

A few years later a shadow – literally – fell over his life in San Remo. The land just beyond the end of his garden was sold, and the new owners began to build a large five-storey hotel. Lear realized at once that his light and his view were going to be completely shut out. He was at first in despair; but in the end friends came to his rescue, and lent him some money to buy another plot of land and build a new villa while waiting for the Villa Emily to be sold. In the autumn of 1881 he moved into the Villa Tennyson, as he called his new home, and remained there until his death at the end of January 1888.

Cheddar Cliffs, 25 August 1849, pen and watercolour. This work and the three reproduced on pp. 22–3 represent the wide range of Lear's travels and his rendering of landscape. *Overleaf: page 22, above,* view of Jerusalem, pen and watercolour, 1858; *page 22, below,* the Ganges at Benares, watercolour, c. 1873: 'One of the most abundantly *bruyant,* and startlingly radiant of places full of bustle and movement'; *page 23,* Monte Generoso, drawing, 14 August 1879.

Maple

green shade

Monte Generoso. P.M.
5.30.
August 14. 1879

*Above left:* Lear with Chichester Fortescue, 1857.

*Above right:* Frances, Countess Waldegrave, lithograph after Swinton.

*Opposite:* W. N. Marstrand's drawing of Edward Lear, 1840.

Throughout his life, Lear was fortunate in his friends. Once he had acquired them, he had the gift of keeping their affection and loyalty until he died. Many of them became influential in public life and were able to help him get commissions, invited him to join them on official travels, and to stay with them when they went *en poste* abroad.

One of the friends to whom he was most deeply attached was Chichester Fortescue, who later became Lord Carlingford. Lear met him in Rome in 1845 when he was twenty-two, that is eleven years younger than Lear himself. He had just left Oxford, and was brought by a friend to Lear's studio. They appear to have taken to one another at once, and met every day until Lear's departure for England a few weeks later. Fortescue noted in his diary: 'He is one of those men of real feeling it is so delightful to meet in this cold-hearted world.' He himself became a Liberal MP, filled many public offices and was awarded a peerage in 1874.

Fortescue was an extremely good-looking young Irishman, highly intelligent and sensitive in his appreciation of art and architecture. Though he could be a most lively, charming and sympathetic companion, with a quick response to Lear's effervescent and whimsical sense of humour, he had a deeply serious and conscientious side to his nature. Lear made a point of seeing him whenever he could, and regularly sent him letters which were among the most delightful he

Edward Lear

nel Luglio 1840.

A caricature of Chichester Fortescue from *Vanity Fair*.

ever wrote. Fortescue answered his letters as diligently, and Lear confessed: 'His society is always, I think invariably, a great comfort to me, and even my boreability and fastidious worry can hardly ever find any vexation therefrom, which I think I cannot say of that of any other living man.' They took a holiday together in Ireland in 1857 to visit Fortescue's relations, an episode which Lear always delighted to recall. A few years later, however, Fortescue married Lady Waldegrave, a prominent hostess, beauty and social charmer of the day, daughter of the famous tenor John Braham. He had been deeply in love with her for many years, and was only waiting for the death of her third husband, a colourless figure by the name of George Harcourt. Lear was warm in his congratulations, and sincerely pleased for his beloved friend, but at the same time the event filled him with sad feelings of loss. Nevertheless both Fortescue and his bride remained among the closest of his circle of friends, and when he read in *The Times* a few years later, while he was in Venice, that Fortescue had been appointed Secretary of State for Ireland, he wrote to Lady Waldegrave:

Being of an undiplomatic and demonstrative nature in matters that give me pleasure, I threw the paper up into the air and jumped aloft myself – ending by taking a small fried whiting out of the plate before me and waving it round my foolish head triumphantly till the tail came off and the body and head flew bounce over to the other side of the table d'hôte room. Then only did I perceive that I was not alone, but that a party was at breakfast in a recess. Happily for me they were not English, and when I made an apology saying I had suddenly seen some good news of a friend of mine, these amiable Italians said – 'Bravissimo, signore! We rejoice with you! And if only we had some little fish we would throw them about the room too, in sympathy with you!' – so we ended by all screaming with laughter.

Lear was in the middle of his Indian tour, in the spring of 1874, when he heard that Fortescue had been created Lord Carlingford for his services to the Liberal Party, and immediately sent him some comic verses of congratulation. He was equally delighted when he was made Lord Privy Seal in 1881, and wrote to him: 'I have never had a clear idea of what the Privy Seal's work really is: and my last notion is that you have continually to superintend seal catching all round the Scotch and English coasts.' From that moment his letters to 40scue (as he addressed him) were filled with comic drawings of seals and jokes about the Great Seal being drawn through the Court on a chain by Fortescue as its guardian, with a 'wallop or flump'.

The friend for whom Lear had the deepest affection, in fact love, was, however, Franklin Lushington. Lear met him in 1849 when staying in Malta with his brother, who was secretary to the Governor. Lushington was a young barrister of twenty-seven. Again, in spite of the disparity in age, they became warm friends at once. Within a week they had left together for a tour of Greece. The expedition was a great success, and Lear noted: 'Mr Lushington has been so constantly the most merry and kind travelling companion.' They toured the whole of the Peloponnese, which Lear had longed for many years to get to know intimately, particularly after his first visit to Athens with Sir Stratford and Lady Canning the year before. He had then travelled on to Macedonia and Albania, and on this occasion, when Lushington had to leave him at the end of April, he went back alone to complete his exploration of southern Albania, in a glow of happiness over his new friendship.

But if Franklin Lushington became eventually even more important to him than Chichester Fortescue, the relationship was not as fortunate. Lushington had a naturally somewhat reserved nature, and as time went on he seemed to grow at least outwardly colder, and incapable of responding to the devotion of a far more sensitive and vulnerable person. Lear once described him as 'a diamond as to value, yet hidden in a tortoise's shell'. At the same time it is clear that, deep down, he felt Lear's friendship to be very precious to him, and even though they had many quarrels, or rather 'misunderstandings', when Lear could no longer bear his taciturnity and lack of warmth, they always made it up. The most difficult time was when Lushington was appointed a judge in Corfu, and Lear went to live on the island in order to be near him. Lushington's responsibilities weighed heavily on him, and made him more difficult for Lear than ever. He wrote to his sister Ann that he sometimes thought he should never have come, and that he had 'hardly known what to do for sheer melancholy sometimes'. Lear was apt to expect too much of his friends; and it was a calamity that the dearest to him of all should have been so unimaginative.

Franklin Lushington: a drawing of c. 1840, by an unknown artist.

It was through Lushington that Lear met the Tennysons, for the poet's sister had married Lushington's brother Edmund. It would seem that for Tennyson himself Lear had more admiration than affection; but his wife Emily became one of his dearest friends, and probably the only person, apart from his sister Ann, to whom he could open his heart about Lushington. After one of his visits to Farringford, in 1859, he wrote to Fortescue: 'I should think, computing moderately, that 15 angels, several hundreds of ordinary women, many philosophers, a heap of truly wise and kind mothers, 3 or 4 minor prophets, and a lot of doctors and schoolmistresses, might all be boiled down, and yet their combined essence fall short of what Emily Tennyson really is.'

Another example of Lear's exceptional gift for establishing close relationships with men a good deal younger than himself was his friendship with Evelyn Baring, later to become famous as the Earl

A drawing of Farringford, Tennyson's home in the Isle of Wight, in 1864.

*Opposite:* Alfred and Emily Tennyson walking in the garden at Farringford with their sons Hallam (right) and Lionel, *c.* 1862, from a photograph by Rejlander.

of Cromer. In spite of the fact that Lushington had become engaged, Lear decided to go back to Corfu for the winter of 1861–2, and it was there that he met Baring, a Royal Artillery subaltern who had been appointed one of the aides to Sir Henry Storks, the new Lord High Commissioner. He was only twenty-one, thirty years younger than Lear, but an immediate mutual attraction seems to have sprung up between them. This friendship with a young, intelligent soldier of lively and sympathetic nature transformed the almost settled melancholy of this period of Lear's life. He wrote him affectionate, amusing, nonsensical letters whenever they were parted; and they left together for Athens when the Ionian Islands were returned to Greek suzerainty in 1864. Lear wrote in his diary: 'Once more I left the loveliest place in the world – with a pang – tho' less this time thro' not being alone.' Nine years later Evelyn Baring, who had become Private Secretary to his cousin Thomas, Lord Northbrook, at that time Viceroy of India, made all the arrangements for Lear's tour of India and Ceylon.

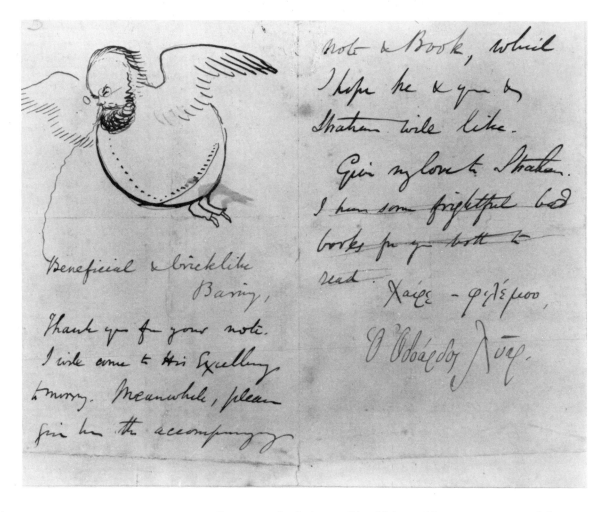

Beneficial & bricklike
    Baring,

Thank you for your note.
I will come to His Excellency
tomorrow. Meanwhile, please
give him the accompanying

note & Book, which
I hope he & you &
Shahen will like.
Give my love to Shahen.
I have some frightful bad
books for you both to
read. Χαῖρε - φιλέμου,
Ο Ουδάρδος Λήρ.

Letter to Evelyn Baring, *c.* 1862–3.

These warmly intimate friendships with young men, and later at San Remo with the boy Hubert Congreve, may lead one to suppose that Lear, a bachelor all his life, was a homosexual. One can only say that this is possible, even probable, especially in view of the well-documented intensity of his feelings for Franklin Lushington; but there is no evidence whatsoever that Lear ever had actual physical relations with any member of his own sex. One must also bear in mind the fact that he did on several occasions contemplate marriage, and appears to have drawn back from the edge more because of doubts about his temperamental suitability than anything else. He was an epileptic, and a perpetual sufferer from asthma and bronchitis; he was abnormally aware of the lack of beauty in his appearance, and as the years went by exaggerated his increasing fatness, the ugliness of his nose and the huge spectacles he had to wear, in the little self-caricaturing sketches with which he adorned his letters; his finances were never secure; but in addition there was something else. During his early years in London, before Knowsley, he had several young cronies with whom he used to make merry and explore the town, among them William Nevill, Bernard Senior and Henry Greening. When the last-named died, Lear wrote in his diary: '*What* days (and *what* nights) we used to share so long ago as 1830 or even earlier. Henry Greening was in those times the life of all our parties, albeit through him partly I got into bad ways.' And in a later entry he admitted having had, about this time, 'every sort of syphilitic disease'. If this is true, and not merely an exaggerated *façon de parler*, he must have been cured in good time, because there is no sign of his having suffered from any dire subsequent effects. Nevertheless such an infection could well have increased his anxiety about marrying.

There are two well-known instances of Lear's at least ostensibly romantic interest in the opposite sex. During his first stay in Corfu, in the middle fifties, he met two young women, Helena and Madeleine Cortazzi, of part Italian, part English parentage, who fascinated him because they were far more cultivated than most of the families in the English colony. Helena in particular attracted him, with her love of Tennyson's poems, many of which she had translated into Italian and even set to music. He felt tempted to propose; then, remembering that he was twenty years older and that neither he nor the girls had any money, hesitated. He returned to England, still hesitating; and when he got back to Corfu the Cortazzis had left. In his depression he wrote to Fortescue: 'If Helena Cortazzi had been here, it would have been useless to think of avoiding asking her to marry me, even had I never so little trust in the wisdom of such a step.' One is inclined to think that this is an obvious case of absence making the heart grow, not fonder perhaps but bolder. If the affair had been more than a flutter, if he had been really serious, he could have made some move, written to Helena at least and kept up the relationship; but he did nothing. He saw her on his next visit to England, and again in Nice some years later; but by then his interest, such as it ever was, had faded.

The other instance was undoubtedly more serious, for one thing because the lady in question was clearly interested in him. In the early sixties, on one of his visits to England, he went to see an old friend, Richard Bethell, who had been created Lord Westbury on being appointed Lord Chancellor. He had been patron as well as friend to Lear, who had known his daughter Augusta from childhood. Now she was grown up, and began to fascinate Lear. He wrote in his diary in 1862: 'Dear little Gussie, who is absolutely good

Evelyn Baring, 1st Earl of Cromer (1841–1917), British Administrator.

Giorgio Cocali in 1881; he died at
Monte Generoso in 1883, after
twenty-seven years in Lear's service.

and sweet and delightful. . . .' In the course of the next few years he
became steadily more obsessed with her – and with the problem of
whether to ask her to marry him. In the event, he put it off and put
it off. Finally she married someone else, tired perhaps of waiting;
the irony was that the man she chose was far more of an invalid
than Lear, in fact completely paralysed. Gussie and Lear remained
affectionate friends; but even when, towards the end of his life, she
was widowed, and came to see him in San Remo showing every
sign of still wanting to be his wife, he could not bring himself to
take the plunge.

It is difficult to conceive that Lear could have made any of his
expeditions to the wilder parts of Europe or the East if he had married early in life. He badly needed someone loyal and devoted who
could be constantly at his side; and he eventually found just the right
person in his Suliot servant, Giorgio Cocali. Giorgio had been born
in Corfu, though his family came from the rock-pinnacle fortress of
Suli in Albania, which had become famous at the beginning of the
century for its heroic stand against the besieging army of the tyrant
Alí Pasha, of whom Byron wrote in a celebrated passage of *Childe
Harold*. Lear engaged him in 1856, and he stayed with Lear for twenty-
seven years until his death in 1883. He coped efficiently with all the
hazards and complications of travel in strange lands, nursing Lear
when he was ill, and quietly, without any fuss, putting things right
when they began to go awry. As time went on Lear, who had grown
somewhat fussy and irritable in his old age, used to explode in
sudden fits of temper with him; but they blew over quickly, and
afterwards Lear always blamed himself. In one of his letters, on his
Indian journey, he was moved to praise Giorgio's 'quiet, content,
and unmurmuring patience, and his constant attention to me, his
often wrong-doing master' – words that reveal the bonds of sensitive
mutual respect and devotion that had grown up between them.
Giorgio was an excellent cook, and was apt to see the world in terms
of the ingredients of food. When he and Lear, on their most adventurous journey, reached the ruined city of Petra in the far Arabian
mountains, Giorgio exclaimed: 'O master, we have come into a
world where everything is made of chocolate, ham, curry powder
and salmon!'

Lear was a tireless writer of letters to his friends and acquaintances,
and used to devote several hours a day, generally in the early morning
before breakfast, to this activity, sometimes sending off as many as
thirty-five letters in one day. It is a thousand pities that, except for
his letters to Fortescue and Lady Waldegrave, to Emily Tennyson
and (in transcript only) to his sister Ann, so very few appear still to
exist – unless they are hidden in private collections. Those that have

survived are the purest and most liberated expression of his affectionate, fun-loving, sharp-witted and totally unpompous nature, and are full of his nonsensical puns and word-coinages, such as 'eggsi stens', 'vorx of hart', 'mental and fizzicle maladies', and flights of extrava-gant fantasy. Sometimes it seems as if he was unable to use an ordinary English word without wanting to give it a nonsensical transformation. 'Do you think there is a Pharmouse or a Nin somewhere near you?' he once wrote to Tennyson when he thought of spending the summer near Farringford. In a letter to Mrs Stuart Wortley, who had bought a drawing of Monte Generoso when he was living in San Remo in

Lear's watercolour of Petra: 'I have found a new world – but my art is helpless to recall it to others, or to represent it to those who have never seen it.'

the last phase of his life, he alleged that another drawing which he enclosed, as a kind of bonus and thank-you, had been done on a journey to the moon, which he proceeded to describe: 'The first view is of the Jizzdoddle rocks, with 2 of the very remarkable planets which surround the moon rising or riz in the distance. These orange coloured and pea green orbs leaving a profound impression of sen-sational surprise on the mind of the spectletator who first beholds them. The second view represents the Rumby-tumby ravine, with the crimson planet Buzz and its 5 Satanites on the horizon. . . .' I find little to choose between these inventions and the modern scientific descriptions brought back from moon-landings: they are equally weird and remote from our daily existence, but Lear's more amusing. Even more extravagantly, he once wrote a letter to his young friend Evelyn Baring in complete, unintelligible nonsense language:

Thrippy Pilliwinx – Inkly tinksy pobblebookle abblesquabs? Flosky? beebul trimble flosky! Okul scratchabibblebongibo, viddle squibble tog-a-tog, ferry-moyassity amsky flamsky ramsky damsky crocklefether squiggs.

Flinkywisty pomm
Slushypipp.

Lear's letters, in spite of the fun with which they are filled and the 'spongetanious' (to use his own remarkable word) expression of his feelings about his friends, reveal how often he was oppressed by the loneliness of his situation. He obviously had moments, as he grew older and witnessed his friends getting married one by one, when he wished that he had been able to marry (though he admitted – no doubt with his unfortunate mother's experience in mind – that the thought of possible yearly additions to his family profoundly dismayed him). He wrote to Fortescue: 'Every marriage of people I care about rather seems to leave me on the bleak shore alone – naturally.' And, with an attempt at stoicism, to Lady Waldegrave: 'As I can't help being alone it is perhaps best to be altogether, jellyfish-fashion, caring for nobody.' Of course that is just what he could not do. Little more than a year before he died, the poet who had given so much pleasure to so many thousands of people, adults as well as children, who had made – and continued to make – all England laugh, wrote: 'My own life seems to me more and more unsatisfactory and melancholy and dark.'

The letters also reveal much about his religious feelings. He began by being a fairly conventional church-goer, often choosing as his reading collections of sermons and the more intelligent religious tracts. As time went on, however, he grew more and more impatient with superficial religious observances and with clerics of all sorts: he was looking for the essential spirit of Christianity, and found

Distant view of Mount Athos from near Leochorio, 21 September 1856.

consolation in his personal belief in 'that Being who disposes of events, and governs futurity'. Going to church on a Sunday morning and listening to the average sermon and watching the fashionable congregation at their devotions began to disgust him as altogether false, and became his *bête noire*. He never became an atheist, but rather something more nearly agnostic. He once wrote: 'We *know* nothing, but is that a reason we should not cling to a hope of reunion after death?' When he visited the monasteries of Mount Athos, he experienced a revulsion that recalls Byron's explosion of rage in the middle of his formal reception by the monks of the monastery he visited in the Ionian Islands, on his way to Missolonghi. 'More pleasing in the sight of the Almighty I really believe, and more like what Jesus Christ intended man to become, is an honest Turk with 6 wives, or a Jew working hard to feed his little old clo' babbies, than these muttering, miserable, mutton-hating, man-avoiding, misogynic, morose and merriment-marring monotoning, many-mule-making, mocking, mournful, minced-fish and marmalade masticating Monx.'

The characteristic flippancy and joking with words does not conceal, but rather accentuates, the violence of his loathing. There were few fixed aversions in Lear's life, but as strong as his revulsion from monks and complacent clerics (and his fear of large dogs) was his dislike of Germans. San Remo was being ruined, he once complained, by an invasion of Germans: 'The ground is all bescattered with horrid Germen, Gerwomen and Gerchildren.'

It is evident that everyone who received a letter from Lear wanted to go on corresponding with him. He devoted so much of his time to writing letters because he so deeply cherished the answers that came to him from his friends. At times, however, the labour seemed almost too much for him. 'I abhor the sight of a pen,' he declared in 1864, 'and if I were an angel I would immediately moult all my quills

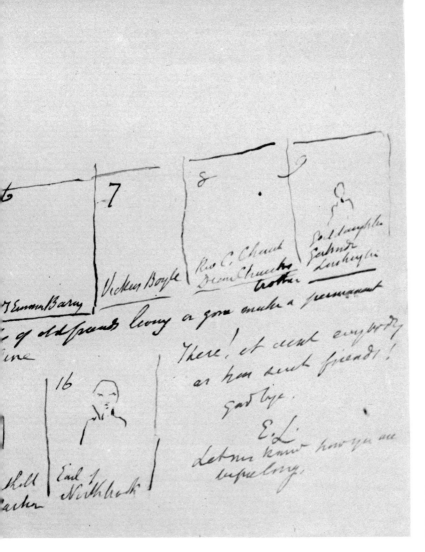

Letter from Lear to Hallam Tennyson, 30 May 1887, with a sketch of the 'picture gallery' of his friends over his fireplace.

for fear of their being used in calligraphy.' In his later years he maintained that he had kept 'specimens' of letters from no less than 'four hundred and forty-four individuals', and once wrote that 'every human being capable of writing ever since the invention of letters must have written to me, with a few exceptions perhaps, such as the prophet Ezekiel, Mary Queen of Scots, and the Venerable Bede'. He had come to the conclusion, he said, that either his friends must be fools or mad, or 'there must be more good qualities about this child than he ever gives or has given himself credit for possessing'. There is no doubt that every single one of his friends would have agreed about the good qualities. After his death, Lushington said of him that the love his friends had felt for him was 'the best and sweetest of garlands that can in spirit be laid on his tomb'.

poky little farm — but we can manage to settle in a 'single man' to furnish a bed, & a roast duck or rabbit. If you think this is not an outrageous idea would you ask him about it — & if you would let me know if he liked to come on Saturday next & at what time, I would meet him at the station;

The Man living here with me is Holman Hunt the Preraphaelite painter — he was the originator of that style, & (let Mr. R. say as he may —) the most original in idea, & the most thoroughly full of understanding concerning poetry of nature & art of any young man I have of late seen. He is very plain & uneducated, except by his

It is perhaps surprising that, with one exception, Lear does not seem to have had any outstanding contemporary painter among his friends. That exception was William Holman Hunt.

When Lear came back, in 1849, for a more prolonged stay in his native country, he took rooms in Stratford Place where he could work and also hold exhibitions of his drawings and paintings. He also enrolled as a student in the Royal Academy Schools, because during his travels in Italy and Greece he had become convinced that he would never reach real excellence as an artist until he had mastered how to draw the human figure. Indeed, he had begun to feel that in more ways than figure-drawing he needed a more thorough grounding in the skills of painting, and some more experienced artist to explain and advise and lead him in the right direction, above all towards the creation of large oil paintings, an ambition which, perhaps unfortunately, obsessed him all his life.

William Holman Hunt, *Our English Coasts*, 1852, painted while he was staying at Clive Vale.

*Opposite:* Letter to Emily Tennyson from Clive Vale farm, 12 October 1852, talking about Holman Hunt and the farm and asking Alfred down for a weekend.

It was just at this time that the Pre-Raphaelite Brotherhood burst upon the jaded London artistic scene, scandalizing all the critics and pundits until Ruskin took up their cause. The original three were Dante Gabriel Rossetti, John Millais and William Holman Hunt. They were already famous when, one day in the summer of 1852, a young enthusiast for their ideals, the painter Robert Martineau, brought Holman Hunt to see Lear's work in his studio in Stratford Place. In his book of memoirs, *Pre-Raphaelitism and the Pre-Raphaelite Brotherhood*, Holman Hunt records the occasion and the close friendship that developed from it: 'Lear overflowed with geniality, and at the same time betrayed anxiety as we turned over the drawings, avowing that he had not the ability to carry out the subjects in oil; in some parts of them he had written in phonetic spelling the character of the points which the outlines would not explain – "Rox", "Korn", "Ski", indulging his love of fun with these vagaries.' (This habit remained with Lear all his life, so that one gets the impression that when he was sketching he was always in happy mood.)

What Hunt saw was sketches made on Lear's travels, 'with little to indicate light or shade', and when Lear told him that his intention was to use these to build up his elaborate oil canvases, Hunt informed

William Holman Hunt in a photograph by Julia Margaret Cameron, 1864.

him bluntly that he was going the wrong way about it. The Pre-Raphaelite motto was 'Back to nature!', and even if the nature that had to be studied was not exactly the same as the subject of the painting, such an open-air substitute had to be found. Lear wanted to build up an oil painting of the Quarries of Syracuse from sketches he had made on the spot. Very well, said Hunt, he knew a landscape in England where all the natural features Lear required could be found, near Hastings in fact. He was just about to leave to do some painting down there himself: would Lear care to join him?

To Lear all this was a revelation, and he was carried away by the practical interest and sympathy his unexpected visitor showed. They decided to take rooms together in some farmhouse; and Hunt would be Lear's artistic adviser. Though it is questionable whether the advice was in fact right, in view of the direction Lear's watercolours were to take and the comparative deadness of the elaborate oil paintings he executed under Hunt's inspiration and methods, nevertheless the friendship and encouragement of an accomplished and innovating fellow-artist was exactly what, psychologically, Lear needed. From that moment, though Hunt was fifteen years his junior, Lear treated him as his master and always called him 'Daddy' or 'Pa'.

The Quarries of Syracuse: *opposite*, one of the original pen and watercolour sketches, 12 June 1847; *below*, the oil painting developed from them, *c.* 1850.

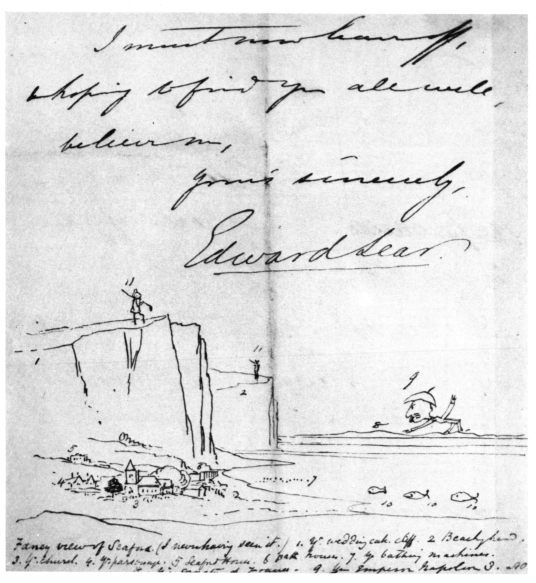

*I must now leave off,*

*whoping to find you all well,*

*believe me,*

*yours sincerely,*

*Edward Lear.*

*Fancy view of Seaford. (I never having seen it.) 1. ye wedding cake cliff. 2 Beachy head.*
*3. ye church. 4. ye parsonage. 5 Seafnt House. 6 park house. 7. ye bathing machines.*
*8. ... coast of France. 9. ye Emperor Napoleon 3. 10*

Sketch of Seaford, from a letter
written by Lear while staying at
Clive Vale farm, 1852; the key
includes the main buildings of the
village, the bathing machines (7),
and the coast of France with
Napoleon (8 and 9).

Hunt gives an amusing picture of Lear at the time when their
friendship started. He was particularly surprised at his terror of dogs.

The Martineaus lived close by, and had at that time a handsome dog called
Caesar, a large Newfoundland, and a great favourite of the family. . . . To Lear, a
man of nearly six feet, with shoulders in width equal to those of Odysseus, the
freaks of this dog were truly exasperating. 'How can the family', said he, 'ask me
to call upon them when they keep a raging animal like that, who has ever his jaws
wide open and his teeth ready to tear helpless strangers to pieces?'

Horses, apparently, were almost as bad, in spite of the fact that he
was to choose to ride them so often on his travels.

While we were at work out of doors he would tell stories of the incidents of his many wanderings, and surprised me by showing that he was uncombative as a tender girl, while at the same time the most indomitable being in encountering danger and hardship. . . . He would rather be killed than fire a pistol or gun; horses he regarded as savage griffins; revolutionists, who were plentiful just then, he looked upon as demons, and Customs officers were the army of Beelzebub. On the other hand, he had the most unquenchable love of the humorous wherever it was found. Recognition of what was ridiculous made him a declared enemy to cant and pretension.

For Lear, the weeks with Holman Hunt at Clive Vale farm were a very happy time. He loved Sussex as much as he loved anywhere in England; he was working hard in an atmosphere of sympathy and mutual understanding; and while he was there many friends came to see him, including Franklin Lushington. What added to his happiness was that the Tennysons were near at hand, at Seaford, where Lear went to visit them. He had long admired the new Laureate's poems, to a large extent because he found his gift for poetic description of landscape almost magical, for ever praising his 'genius for the perception of the beautiful in landscape'. He felt that he himself had a special aptitude for translation of the poetry into painting, and conceived the ambitious project of preparing a grand pictorial edition of the poems, with 124 illustrations in line and colour. He wrote to Emily, who persuaded the poet to agree, and Lear set to work with enthusiasm on a task that, on and off, was to occupy him for thirty-five years, and was by no means finished at his death.

In addition Lear, though he does not seem to have had any training in music, had a modest but by no means negligible gift for composing songs, and made settings of several of Tennyson's lyrics. He became very popular as an after-dinner performer, and when he sang these settings, to his own accompaniment, 'with little voice, but with intense feeling and individuality', as we are told, he would often bring tears to the eyes of his audience. The professional musicians were apt to turn up their noses, but on one occasion, Lear tells us himself, when he sang his setting of 'Home they brought her warrior dead' at a party at John Millais's house in Cromwell Place, the Dean of Carlisle in a broken voice exclaimed: 'Sir, you ought to have half the Laureateship!' I do not think that Tennyson himself was present.

In spite of his social popularity, and the fact that he was having luck in selling his paintings (*The Quarries of Syracuse* was accepted for the Royal Academy and sold to Earl Beauchamp), this was the last occasion on which Lear spent any length of time in England. The English climate was getting him down again, his health was deteriorating, and at the beginning of December 1853 he left for a tour of Egypt. He came back briefly in the spring, and made a tour of Switzerland in the summer. He appears to have decided to give

Self-caricature from a letter of unknown date addressed on the reverse to 'E. Baring, ADC. The Palace', showing Lear seated at the piano; pen and ink on blue paper.

*Above:* 'L[ear] sets out from the house of Captn. Hornby, R.N.', one of a series of eight drawings probably done in the mid 1830s. The scene is Greenwich; Lear punningly draws the conveyance in which he travelled (hackney coach or 'fly') as an actual fly. Hornby was a grandson of the twelfth Earl of Derby.

*Right:* A sketch by Lear of himself at the Royal Academy Schools with a skeleton leaning over him, from a letter written to Chichester Fortescue in January 1850: 'I tried with 51 little boys and 19 of us were admitted. I go with a large book and a piece of chalk to school every day like a good little boy.'

England another chance, but the winter of 1854–5 was even worse for his health, and his bronchial troubles were so bad that he hardly went out at all. Meanwhile Lushington had been appointed Judge to the Supreme Court in the Ionian Islands, and it was decided that Lear should accompany him to Corfu. They left towards the end of November 1855. No more English winters, ever again, for Lear.

At about this time, soon before or soon after his fortieth birthday, Lear began to grow the bushy beard which was a feature of all later portraits, photographs and caricature drawings which he made of himself. In the amusing series of sketches he drew in the mid-thirties of a visit paid to Captain Hornby RN (a grandson of the Earl of Derby) at Greenwich, he portrays himself as very lanky and thin and entirely beardless. His face is equally beardless, but adorned with a pencil moustache, in the well-known drawing by Marstrand of 1840. In the comic sketch of himself working in the Academy Schools with a skeleton leaning over him, in approximately 1849–50, he is the same; but by 1857, when Holman Hunt made a drawing of him, he was already sporting the beard. One may guess that it was about the same period that he began markedly to put on weight, though it seems unlikely that with his continual activity he was ever anything like as 'perfectly spherical' as he jokingly pretended.

From a letter to Emily Tennyson, 14 June 1861. Lear's picture of Masada on the Dead Sea was seven feet long.

MASADA . on the
dead sea - -
nink case.
not to be jumped on

Oatlands Parcotel .
Waltnontems. Surry.
Jany. 14/1861

My dear Mrs Tennyson,
As you see by the above illustration, I ha—
— — it my large picture of Masada —

There was an Old Derry down Derry, who loved to see little folks merry;
So he made them a Book, and with laughter they shook
At the fun of that Derry down Derry.

The title page of *A Book of Nonsense*, 1846.

Lear's first collection of limericks, which appeared in 1846 under the title of *A Book of Nonsense*, was attributed to 'Derry down Derry, who loved to see little folks merry', and the major part of it did in fact consist of the rhymes with which he had delighted the little Stanley children at Knowsley. To each of the limericks he added one of his inimitable nonsense drawings; they were probably more carefully worked repetitions of the original impromptu pen-and-ink illustrations thrown off for the children, and were reproduced by lithography. The book was a great success, and in 1861 he published an enlarged edition, this time under his own name, in which the drawings were reproduced by means of wood-engravings executed under his supervision. *A Book of Nonsense* went into thirty editions during his lifetime.

Naturally, in the years before Lear acknowledged the book, people wanted to know who the author was. Many rumours circulated, many wild guesses were made – which continued even after his name appeared on the title page. The most ingenious and preposterous supposition of all only came to Lear's knowledge by chance. He describes how he was travelling by train from London to Guildford one day, when two little boys, accompanied by two ladies, entered the carriage with a copy of the *Book of Nonsense*, which they proceeded to read aloud from and crow over. An old gentleman who was in the same carriage thereupon remarked: 'How grateful all children and parents ought to be to the statesman who has given his time to composing that charming book!' The ladies looked puzzled, and pointed out that the name on the title page was EDWARD LEAR. The old gentle-man immediately replied that that was only a little bit of fun on the part of the Earl of Derby: Edward was his Christian name, and LEAR was merely an anagram of EARL. The ladies, unconvinced, showed him the dedication to 'the great-grandchildren, grand-nephews and grand-nieces of Edward, thirteenth Earl of Derby, by the author, Edward Lear'. 'Simply a piece of mystification!' replied the old gentleman. 'I can inform you, no such person as "Edward Lear" exists.'

Lear goes on: 'Hitherto I had kept silence, but as my hat was, as well as my handkerchief and stick, largely marked inside with my name, and as I happened to have in my pocket several letters addressed to me, the temptation was too great to resist, so, flashing all these articles at once on my would-be extinguisher's attention, I speedily reduced him to silence.'

In 1871 he published another volume, which he called *Nonsense Songs, Stories, Botany and Alphabets*. This second book contained the first of his nonsense *poems*, 'The Owl and the Pussy-cat' and 'The Jumblies'. The story is that the former was written in the winter

Lear proves to the disbeliever in the railway carriage that the author of the *Book of Nonsense* really exists.

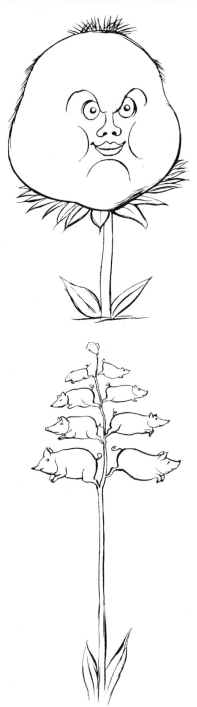

*Phattfacia Stupenda (top)* and
*Piggiwiggia Pyramidalis*, plates from
*Nonsense Songs, Stories, Botany and
Alphabets*, 1871.

of 1868 for Janet Symonds, the three-year-old daughter of John Addington Symonds, who was staying with her father at Cannes. It was always children who inspired him: the next source of inspiration came from a small boy called Hubert Congreve, the son of a school-master who had taught at Rugby and had come out to San Remo in a vain attempt to save the lives of his sick wife and an older son. Lear, who had made friends with his father, met the boy one day in the autumn of 1869, and according to Hubert Congreve's own account, written many years later as an introduction to the second volume of Lady Strachey's edition of the letters, 'Lear at once asked me if I knew who he was, and without waiting for a reply pro-ceeded to tell me a long, nonsense name, compounded of all the languages he knew.' The young Hubert came to adore Lear, whom he called 'my dearest and best friend of the older generation', and the feeling was reciprocated by Lear. It was almost certainly for Hubert that he began to write his nonsense botany, with its extremely peculiar punning plants (all illustrated) such as the Nasticreechia Krorluppia, the Piggiwiggia Pyramidalis and the Phattfacia Stupenda. It is also likely that the nonsense cookery was invented for Hubert, for when the Congreves were invited to dine with him he would send a non-sense menu ahead with recipes such as that for Gosky Patties:

To Make Gosky Patties.
Take a Pig, three or four years of age, and tie him by the off hind leg to a post. Place 5 pounds of currants, 3 of sugar, 2 pecks of peas, 18 roast chestnuts, a candle and 6 bushels of turnips, within his reach; if he eats these, constantly provide him with more. Then procure some cream, some slices of Cheshire cheese, four quires of foolscap paper, and a packet of black pins. Work the whole into a paste, and spread it out to dry on a sheet of clean brown water-proof linen. When the paste is perfectly dry, but not before, proceed to beat the Pig violently, with the handle of a large broom. If he squeals, beat him again. Visit the paste and beat the Pig alternately for some days, and ascertain if at the end of that period the whole is about to turn into Gosky Patties. If it does not then, it never will; and in that case the Pig may be let loose, and the whole process may be considered as finished.

Lear hoped for some time that Hubert might become an artist, gave him drawing lessons, and took him out on sketching expeditions, of which Hubert has given us a vivid glimpse:

Lear plodding slowly along, old George following behind, laden with lunch and drawing materials. When we came to a good subject, Lear would sit down, and taking his block from George, would lift his spectacles, and gaze for several minutes at the scene through a monocular glass he always carried; then, laying down the glass, and adjusting his spectacles, he would put on paper the view before us, mountain range, villages and foreground, with a rapidity and accuracy that inspired me with awestruck admiration.

Cockatooca
Superba.

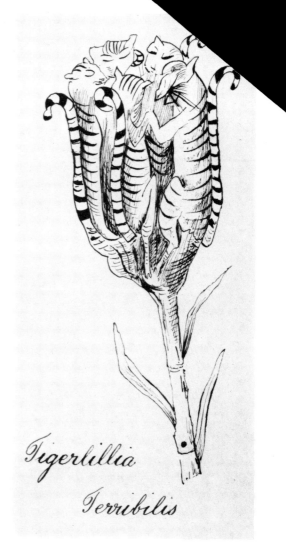

Tigerlillia
Terribilis

For the second volume of nonsense, Lear's publisher had advised him to leave his limericks out. He had been pouring them out all the time, and they appeared a year later in his third volume, *More Nonsense, Pictures, Rhymes, Botany*. By this time his fame as a nonsense-writer had spread far and wide, and he was making money out of his books. The new volume was immediately successful, and he wrote to Chichester Fortescue: 'It is queer (and you would say so if you saw me), that I am the man as is making some three or four thousand people laugh in England all at one time.' The last volume to appear in his lifetime was *Laughable Lyrics*, which was published in 1877 and contains some of the most famous of his poems, including

Two original drawings, *c.* 1870, for *Nonsense Botany*.

'And the dish ran away with the spoon . . .', an original nonsense drawing, *c*. 1860.

'The Courtship of the Yonghy-Bonghy-Bò' and 'The Dong with a luminous Nose'. A sad footnote to this tale of success was that the printer-publisher who had brought out the last three of his nonsense books, Robert Bush, went bankrupt in June 1880, owing Lear a considerable sum of money and in addition reporting that he had lost all the blocks.

One of the most interesting unanswered questions of literary history is whether Edward Lear and Lewis Carroll read one another's works or were in any way influenced by one another. There is no mention of either in the other's diaries or letters, as far as we have them. Lear was undoubtedly the first on the scene, for *Alice in Wonderland* did not appear until 1865, and *Through the Looking Glass* seven years later, in 1872. Lewis Carroll published no limericks, and his brand of nonsense is undoubtedly more intellectual, concealing riddles and logical puzzles in a way totally alien to Edward Lear, who, on his side, has a vein of tender and often melancholic feeling that is nowhere to be found in Carroll's *Alice* books, though both originally wrote for children. Nevertheless it is perhaps not too fanciful to see a certain, possibly distant consanguinity between Lear's songs and such poems by Carroll as ''Tis the Voice of the Lobster', 'Beautiful Soup' (though both were of course parodies) and 'Jabberwocky'.

Lear's nonsense poetry, by the comic absurdity of its statement, has given delight to countless thousands of readers, adults as well as the children for whom it was originally written; and one feels inclined to leave it at that. All nonsense, whether by Lear or Carroll or any one of their numerous modern successors, is a parody or standing-on-its-head of the strict and rational world in which we have to live, and so momentarily releases us from its chains. The argument doesn't make sense: it is in fact non-sense. Nevertheless, in examining Lear's poetry a little more closely, one may understand better the various skills he employed, and the sources in his own mind and temperament out of which it arose; that is, one may understand Lear himself better.

There is no norm for the limerick, except the pattern Lear – or perhaps one should say the author of 'There was a sick man of Tobago' – adopted. That is, two three-beat lines which rhyme, followed by two two-beat lines (sometimes written as one) which also rhyme, and concluded by a fifth which rhymes with the first two, the whole enclosing a nonsensical argument or statement:

*There was an Old Man who supposed*
*That the street door was partially closed;*
*But some very large rats*
*Ate his coats and his hats,*
*While that futile old gentleman dozed.*

This illustration and the next seven are all from *A Book of Nonsense*, 1861 edition.

Lear is particularly fond of an 'Old Man' or 'Old Person' as the subject of his limericks, though he occasionally uses the alternative of 'Young Lady' or 'Young Person':

*There was a Young Person of Crete*
*Whose toilette was far from complete;*
  *She dressed in a sack,*
  *Spickle-speckled with black,*
*That ombliferous person of Crete.*

Here he indulges his fondness for words invented by himself. No one knows what 'ombliferous' means, any more than 'runcible' or 'scroobious', words he was also particularly fond of; but it sounds most nonsensically appropriate to the eccentric young person of Crete.

Most of the time Lear is content to repeat the first line as the last, with only a slight variation; but sometimes (as in my first example) he uses the last line to develop and clinch the argument:

*There was an Old Man who said 'Hush!*
*I perceive a young bird in this bush!'*
  *When they said – 'Is it small?'*
  *He replied – 'Not at all!*
*It is four times as big as the bush!'*

Philosophically minded devotees of Lear have found a concealed metaphysical observation in some of the limericks:

*There was an Old Man who said, 'Well!*
*Will nobody answer this bell?*
  *I have pulled day and night,*
  *Till my hair has grown white,*
*But nobody answers this bell!'*

– which may be considered, symbolically and nonsensically, to contain the same reflection on the riddle of the universe as Omar Khayyám's stanza:

In Lear's limericks 'they' play a very dubious role. Most of the time they are censorious, conventional and vindictive, interfering in innocent pleasures if they are in the least unusual. One cannot help feeling that in these limericks Lear is giving vent to contempt and disgust for officious, busybodying people through the violence with which he portrays their behaviour:

*There was an Old Man of Whitehaven,*
*Who danced a quadrille with a Raven;*
*But they said – 'It's absurd*
*To encourage this bird!'*
*So they smashed that Old Man of Whitehaven.*

'They' were equally offended by the Old Man of Thermopylae, who never did anything properly and who boiled eggs in his shoes, warning him that if he continued with this reprehensible habit they would drive him out of Thermopylae; and 'they' also objected to the Old Man of Dumblane, because his long legs made him look like a crane. One remembers that Lear had unusually long legs; but his chief obsession was with the size of his nose. This emerges again and again, long before he had written of the 'Dong with a luminous Nose', as in:

*There was an Old Man, on whose nose*
*Most birds of the air could repose;*
  *But they all flew away,*
  *At the closing of day,*
*Which relieved that Old Man and his nose.*

One may equally, of course, interpret these noses, which extend to enormous length and are put to the strangest uses, as the unconscious phallic images of a sexually repressed man; but it seems to me that their grotesquely comic effect, for children at least, is in no way diminished by such psychoanalytical interpretation.

Lear was obviously very fond of birds, not only the parrots with the drawing of which he chose to begin his career, but also owls, ravens, rooks and all the other 'birds in the air' which almost always play a sympathetic role in his work:

*There was a Young Lady whose bonnet*
*Came untied when the birds sate upon it;*
  *But she said, 'I don't care!*
  *All the birds in the air*
*Are welcome to sit on my bonnet!'*

However comic, fantastic and inconsequential the limericks are, they would be far less so in their total effect without the drawings with which Lear regularly accompanied them: it is in the combination that his unique genius lies. The drawing which accompanies the above limerick is not only an exquisitely designed piece of work,

but also miraculous in its purity of line and free lyricism — at a time when most drawing in England was painstakingly the opposite. It is especially interesting to note the pointed toes of the Young Lady: in Lear's nonsense drawings again and again the chief characters point their toes as in ballet. There is a sense of dance everywhere in these drawings, as there is so often in the verses themselves. Even the Old Man of Apulia, who 'fed twenty sons/Upon nothing but buns', has his left foot pointed as he offers the buns to his progeny. One cannot help wondering whether, in those early London years of which we know so little, Lear may perhaps have frequented the performances of famous dancers such as Taglioni, Ellsler and Vestris, put on with such *éclat* in the London theatres at that period, and become an early balletomane. As the Old Man of Whitehaven danced with the Raven, so the Old Person of Filey, to take one of many other examples, 'danced perfectly well/To the sound of a bell', and

*There was an Old Man of Apulia*
*Whose conduct was very peculiar.*
*He fed twenty sons*
*Upon nothing but buns,*
*That whimsical man of Apulia.*

*There was an Old Person of Skye,*
*Who waltz'd with a Bluebottle fly:*
*They buzzed a sweet tune*
*To the light of the moon,*
*And entranced all the people of Skye.*

What is particularly interesting about the drawing to this limerick is the likeness of the Bluebottle fly and his partner. The Old Person, the enormous size of whose spectacles matches the enormous eyes of the fly, seems to be becoming a fly himself, for his swallow-tail coat bears a most curious resemblance to the folded wings of the bluebottle; it is almost a wing-case. This process of empathy can also be seen at work in the drawing of the Old Man who said 'Hush!', for he has become almost as avian in appearance as the young bird he is regarding with such astonishment.

In the original title-page drawing for the first edition of the *Book of Nonsense*, the 'little folks' are leaping about in an ecstasy of joy. Such frenzy is characteristic of nearly all the background figures, young and old, in the limericks, who throw themselves about, flinging their arms in the air with total abandon. Their animation and violence of reaction – as in the case of the Young Lady whose eyes

*Were unique as to colour and size;*
*When she opened them wide,*
*People all turned aside,*
*And started away in surprise*

*Opposite above:*
*There was an Old Man of Peru,*
*Who watched his wife making a stew,*
*Till once by mistake,*
*In a stove she did bake*
*That unfortunate man of Peru.*
Original drawing for *A Book of Nonsense*, 1846.

*Opposite below:* The plate, by Lear, for the 1861 edition of *A Book of Nonsense*, showing evident alterations to the drawing.

– is in curious contrast to the calm of Lear's watercolours, which seem to belong to an entirely different range of feeling: only in the last phase of his career did he show the sea, which occurs as a background in so many, as anything but smooth and unruffled. There is nevertheless very little that could frighten a child in the limerick illustrations as published: if there is cruelty it is equally matched with absurdity, so that a child will normally laugh. This is not always the case, however, with the original rough drawings, some of which have survived and have been published in *Lear in the Original*. For instance, the wife of the Old Man of Peru, who baked him by mistake in a stew, has an expression of fiendish savagery on her face which makes one wonder whether the action was altogether by mistake. This is much toned down in the published version. In the same book there is an unpublished illustration by Lear to a verse in Anne Lindsay's 'Auld Robin Grey':

*My mother did not speak*
*But she looked in my face till my heart was like to break . . .*

There was an old man of Peru, who watched his wife making a stew,
Till once by mistake, in a stove she did bake, that unfortunate man of Peru

22

*My mother did not speak
But she looked in my face, till my heart was like to break!*

*Above:* A slightly altered quotation from the ballad 'Auld Robin Gray', by Anne Lindsay, is the inspiration for this drawing. The one opposite, similarly dated November 1841, illustrates the same poem.

in which the mother has an altogether terrifying presence and expression. Sometimes, one feels, Lear may have had to keep a very close censorship on the emotions that welled up from his subconscious. And sometimes in his verses, too, one finds him approaching the wilder shores of surrealism, as in this unfinished poem:

> *Mrs Jaypher found a wafer*
> *Which she stuck upon a note;*
> *This she took and gave the cook.*
> *Then she went and bought a boat*
> *Which she paddled down the stream*
> *Shouting: 'Ice produces cream,*
> *Beer when churned produces butter!*
> *Henceforth all the words I utter*
> *Distant ages thus shall note –*
> *From the Jaypher Wisdom-Boat. . . .'*

It is difficult not to come to the conclusion that one would have been extremely frightened if one had met Mrs Jaypher on the river of a summer's afternoon.

There was an Old Person of Harrow
Who bought a mahogany barrow,
    For he said to his wife
     'You're the joy of my life!
And I'll wheel you all day in this barrow!'

Overleaf: *L.E.A.R.*, four letters from
a nonsense alphabet, *c.* 1880.

# L l L l

L was a very small Lamp,
It was lighted every night;
And whereas before, the room was dark,
It made that room quite light

# E e E e

E was a beautiful Eagle,
Whose head was completely white;
He sate and looked at the sun all day,
And was fast asleep all night.

# A a a A

A was a lovely Apple
  which was very red & round,
~~And when~~ It tumbled off an Apple tree
  And fell upon the ground.

# R r R r

R was a Rat – His tail was long,
But he stole Some bread,
  Which was Certainly wrong.

'The Owl and the Pussy-cat', from *Nonsense Songs, Stories, Botany and Alphabets*, 1871.

Some time in the 1860s, after his wanderings in Calabria, Greece and Albania and the Holy Land were over, Lear began to write a different kind of nonsense poetry, more ambitious and more original than the limericks – those songs for which he is most cherished and most lovingly remembered. They are a kind of transposed Romantic poetry, written with remarkable skill, with a sense of rhythmic architecture and word music that recalls the masters, especially his beloved Tennyson. They are not parodies, for they have an under-tone of deep feeling that hints at the troubles of Lear's own emotional life, but a new mixture: one revels in the inconsequential play of the imagination while one responds to the counterpointing sadness and heartbreak. His invented places, 'the Hills of the Chankly Bore' and 'the great Gromboolian plain', have a resonance as profound as that of Shelley's 'wild Carmanian waste' and 'lone Chorasmian shore'. The result is that, if you succumb to the incantation, if you don't pull yourself up and examine the sense, you are almost ready to accept the poems in which they appear as examples of the great Romantic tradition.

The earliest of these songs, as I have already mentioned, appeared in Lear's second book of nonsense, published in 1871, *Nonsense Songs, Stories, Botany and Alphabets*, and it seems likely that the first of all to be written was the one that is probably still the greatest favourite, 'The Owl and the Pussy-cat':

*The Owl and the Pussy-cat went to sea*
  *In a beautiful pea-green boat,*
*They took some honey, and plenty of money*
  *Wrapped up in a five-pound note.*
*The Owl looked up to the stars above,*
  *And sang to a small guitar,*
*'O lovely Pussy! O Pussy, my love,*
  *What a beautiful Pussy you are,*
      *You are,*
      *You are!*
  *What a beautiful Pussy you are!'*

Nothing could be more light-heartedly nonsensical and captivating, nor could a happier end be devised:

*And hand in hand, on the edge of the sand,*
  *They danced by the light of the moon,*
      *The moon,*
      *The moon,*
  *They danced by the light of the moon.*

One feels that this song must have come out of a particularly happy moment in Lear's life. The same mood permeates 'The Duck and the Kangaroo', and 'The Jumblies' with its magical chorus:

'The Jumblies', from *Nonsense Songs, Stories, Botany and Alphabets*, 1871.

*Far and few, far and few,*
  *Are the lands where the Jumblies live;*
*Their heads are green, and their hands are blue,*
  *And they went to sea in a sieve.*

Like the Owl and the Pussy-cat and the Duck and the Kangaroo, and even Mr Daddy Long-legs and Mr Floppy Fly (who appear to have been the first of Lear's creatures to reach the 'great Gromboolian plain'), the Jumblies found solace and fulfilment in a long voyage beyond the limits of the known world (even though they came back, unlike the little creatures of 'Calico Pie'). One cannot help feeling that Lear himself, forever setting forth upon yet another long journey, had a dream of pushing out one day beyond the names in the atlas.

When we come to the songs in the 1877 volume, *Laughable Lyrics*, a new note makes itself heard. It is true that in 'The Pobble Who Has No Toes' and 'The Quangle Wangle's Hat' the happy mood of 'all's well that ends well' reappears; but through the nonsensical trappings and absurd *dramatis personae* (and the equally absurd drawings which accompany them) of 'The Courtship of the Yonghy-Bonghy-Bò' and 'The Dong with a luminous Nose', one is aware of a theme of personal sadness and desolation, at moments so strong that one is on the verge of tears in the midst of one's laughter. Is it far-fetched to see, in the proposal of the Yonghy-Bonghy-Bò and Lady Jingly Jones's reply, a parable of Lear's own failure to find the perfect person to love and live with him, even though one does not necessarily have to identify Lady Jingly too closely with Gussie Bethell?

'Calico Pie', from *Nonsense Songs, Stories, Botany and Alphabets*, 1871; and *opposite*, 'The Courtship of the Yonghy-Bonghy-Bò', from *Laughable Lyrics*, 1877.

'On this Coast of Coromandel
   Shrimps and watercresses grow,
      Prawns are plentiful and cheap,'
   Said the Yonghy-Bonghy-Bò.
'You shall have my chairs and candle,
And my jug without a handle! –
      Gaze upon the rolling deep
      (Fish is plentiful and cheap)
      As the sea, my love is deep!'
   Said the Yonghy-Bonghy-Bò,
   Said the Yonghy-Bonghy-Bò.

Lady Jingly answered sadly,
   And her tears began to flow, –
      'Your proposal comes too late,
   Mr Yonghy-Bonghy-Bò!
I would be your wife most gladly!'
(Here she twirled her fingers madly,)
      'But in England I've a mate!
      Yes! you've asked me far too late,
      For in England I've a mate,
   Mr Yonghy-Bonghy-Bò!
   Mr Yonghy-Bonghy-Bò!'

'The Dong' is the most richly orchestrated of the songs in the 1877 volume, perhaps the most richly orchestrated of all Lear's songs, and the one in which he shows his poetic skill at its highest by creating a menacing, doom-laden atmosphere by a combination of verbal effects and sonorous images of wild nature worthy of Tennyson himself:

> When awful darkness and silence reign
> Over the great Gromboolian plain,
>   Through the long, long wintry nights; –
> When the angry breakers roar
> As they beat on the rocky shore; –
>   When storm-clouds brood on the towering heights
> Of the Hills of the Chankly Bore. . . .

This macabre Romantic fantasia is the dark pendant to 'The Jumblies', using the same chorus but this time to emphasize the Dong's desolation and sense of abandonment. To balance the heightened emotional mood, Lear invents the most ludicrous of all his nonsense creatures, the most fearsome and at the same time the funniest emanation from his subconscious of his sense of personal physical repulsiveness:

*And now each night, and all night long,*
*Over those plains still roams the Dong;*
*And above the wail of the Chimp and Snipe*
*You may hear the squeak of his plaintive pipe*
*While ever he seeks, but seeks in vain*
*To meet with his Jumbly Girl again;*
*Lonely and wild – all night he goes, –*
*The Dong with a luminous Nose!*
*And all who watch at the midnight hour,*
*From Hall or Terrace, or lofty Tower,*
*Cry, as they trace the Meteor bright,*
*Moving along through the dreary night, –*
*'This is the hour when forth he goes,*
*The Dong with a luminous Nose!*
*Yonder – over the plain he goes;*
*He goes!*
*He goes;*
*The Dong with a luminous Nose!'*

It is pointless to regret that a man so sensitive to the music of words, and with such poetic skill at his command, never wrote a poem to which laughter is not an essential part of our reaction. 'The Dong with a luminous Nose' is likely to last as long, and will continue to bewitch our imagination as powerfully, as any poem of serious intent; unless in the future we were ever to reach a stage where we were born grown up, without having known the wonder-world of childhood where even the Pobble who has no Toes and the Quangle-Wangle are possible.

*There was an Old Man of Carlisle,*
*Who was left on a desolate isle:*
*Where he fed upon cakes,*
*And lived wholly with snakes,*
*Who danced with that man of Carlisle.*

A nineteenth-century engraving of Osborne House, designed by Prince Albert and Thomas Cubitt.

In 1841 Lear published his *Views in Rome and its Environs*, which consisted of lithographs taken from his drawings, but no text to speak of. His first book with text as an account of his travels was *Illustrated Excursions in Italy*, which was published in 1846 in two volumes. It had the unexpected result of an invitation from Queen Victoria, twenty-seven years old at the time, to give her lessons in drawing.

The lessons started at Osborne in July, and the Queen noted in her diary on the 15th: 'Had a drawing lesson from Mr Lear, who sketched before me and teaches remarkably well, in landscape painting in watercolours.' One could wish that Lear's own account of these lessons had survived; we know that he wrote one down, but no trace has been found. Later, in his letters, he recalled two episodes, which probably took place when the lessons were resumed at Buckingham Palace. He got on excellently with the Queen, but, not unnaturally, was ignorant of the finer points of etiquette. Like many others in those days when the heating of rooms was done entirely by open fires, he liked warming his coat-tails on the hearthrug. Seeing a blazing fire one day when only he and a Lord-in-Waiting were in the room with the Queen, he immediately went and placed himself in front of it. This was an innocent breach of etiquette; the Lord-in-Waiting tried tactfully to draw him away to look at a painting or some other object, but again and again Lear, perfectly insouciant, returned to his place on the hearthrug. Only later was his mistake explained to him. Again, one day, the Queen, who had evidently found Lear very sympathetic as well as a good drawing master, began to show him some of the cases containing the priceless Royal collection of miniatures. 'Oh, where *did* you get all these beautiful things?' exclaimed Lear, completely carried away. The Queen replied, gently but with dignity: 'I inherited them, Mr Lear.'

The text which accompanied the first volume of *Illustrated Excursions in Italy* (the second had only brief notes) gave a foretaste of Lear's inimitable style as a travel writer, which was to come to full flower in the three subsequent books on southern Italy, Albania and Greece, and Corsica. On the journeys described in this first volume he and one of his friends from Rome, Charles Knight, penetrated on horseback to the remotest parts of the Abruzzi, one of the wildest regions of Italy which seemed as if forgotten by civilization, and lived rough, spending the nights (except when put up by local dignitaries) in the almost unbearable discomfort of filthy and chaotic village inns. His historical sense, as always, could not be submerged by the miseries of circumstance. Surveying the Lake of Fucino, near Avezzano, he wrote:

A herd of white goats blinking and sneezing lazily in the early sun; their goatherd piping on a little reed; two or three large falcons soaring above the Lake; the watchful cormorant sitting motionless on its shining surface; and a host of merry flies sporting in the fragrant air, – these were the only signs of life in the very spot where the thrones of Claudius and his Empress were placed on the crowd-blackened hill: a few distant fishing-boats dotted the Lake where, eighteen centuries ago, the cries of combat rent the air, and the glitter of contending galleys delighted the Roman multitude. . . .

On one occasion, because his passport had the usual preliminary flourish signed by the British Foreign Secretary, a village policeman who examined it thought that Lear was Palmerston himself – at that time hated by the official classes in the Monarchist regions south of Rome because of his proclaimed support for the Liberals – and dragged him off triumphantly as a supreme prize, until they met the Sott'Intendente, who released him with many apologies. 'Some have greatness thrust upon them,' was Lear's comment.

The *Journals of a Landscape Painter in Southern Calabria and the Kingdom of Naples*, to give it its full name, was published in 1852, *after* the Albanian book, but described journeys actually undertaken before, in 1847. Lear set out for Calabria at the end of July with

Queen Victoria in 1846.

another young student of painting he had met in Rome. John Proby was eleven years younger than Lear; during the late spring they had visited Sicily together, but it was only on the Calabrian journey that Lear discovered he was really Lord John Proby, heir to the Earl of Carysfort. He found him at times 'imperious and contradictory', which, when he became aware of the young man's rank, he felt had to be excused; though he wrote to Ann that if he had known of it he would never have asked Proby to accompany him. They quarrelled; they made it up; and Lear thereafter regretted his irritability and called him 'of the best creatures possible'. When he died ten years later, Lear was full of remorse and regrets.

What is most striking about the book is the remarkably fresh and lively way it is written, communicating a sense of continuous zestful enjoyment. The descriptions of places have a vivid charm, and absurd happenings *en route* and eccentric persons encountered are brought before us with engaging humour.

Lear engaged a Calabrian servant, Ciccio, and when he explained to him the plan of their travels, going straight ahead or stopping to sketch whenever it pleased him, the reply was simply the incomprehensible sentence: 'Dógo; díghi, dóghi, dághi, dà,' repeated on every possible occasion thereafter. This caused Lear and his companion great merriment. One cannot help thinking that it was the recollection of Ciccio's refrain that inspired the creation, later on, of the Yonghy-Bonghy-Bò.

Lear and John Proby, on their expedition to Sicily, are 'pursued through the streets by an ineffable multitude of rabid mendicants': a sketch made in Trapani, 16 May 1847.

A characteristic example of the kind of accommodation they found – and apparently cheerfully endured – in the villages where they had to spend the night is found in the account of Condufori:

The wretched hut we were in was more than half choked up by the bed of a sick man, with barrels, many calf-skins filled with wine, and a projecting stone fire-place; moreover, it was as dark as Erebus; so in the palpable obscure I sat down on a large live pig, who slid away, to my disgust, from under me, and made a portentous squeaking, to the disquiet of a horde of fowls, perched on every available spot above and below. The little light the place rejoiced in was disturbed by a crowd of thirty or forty 'Turchi' who glared at us with the utmost curiosity, and talked in their vernacular tongue without ceasing.

In another village, Stignano, a more uncloudedly entertaining incident is recorded:

The most remarkable accident during our stay was caused by a small juvenile Caristò, who, during the mid-day meal, climbed abruptly on to the table, and before he could be rescued, performed a series of struggles among the dishes, which ended by the little pickle's losing his balance and collapsing suddenly in a sitting posture into the very middle of the macaroni dish, from which P. and I rejoiced to think we had been previously helped. One sees in Valentines Cupids on beds of roses, or birds' nests; but a slightly clothed Calabrese infant sitting in the midst of a hot dish of macaroni appears to me a perfectly novel idea.

Scilla, Calabria: '. . . one of the most striking bits of coast scenery, its white buildings and massive castled crag standing out in noble relief against the dark blue waves'. This illustration and the next three are from *Journals of a Landscape Painter in Southern Calabria*, 1852.

His response to the beauty of natural scenery, his unfailing joy in discovering new landscapes and vistas, which was surely the chief motor that drove him on untiringly to ever new explorations under conditions that would have defeated most other travellers – particularly those who were semi-invalids, as Lear always was – is well illustrated by his entry about the approach to Pietrapennata on the early morning of 5 August:

How exquisite was the sweet morning light and air – the deep ravine full of ilex, the mill, and the ascent to the opposite side, where those surpassing woods fringed the park-like glades, or formed magnificent pictures with their grey trunks, and arms flung out over rock and dell! O rare woods of Pietrapennata! I do not remember to have seen a lovelier spot than the 'winged rock' – not unaptly named, feathered as it is from base to summit. None of your dense carpet-forests – your monotonies of verdure, but made up of separate combinations of pictorial effect, such as one can hardly fancy – Claude and Salvator Rosa at every step! All the morning we drew in this beautiful place, and little enough could our utmost efforts make of what would occupy a regiment of landscape-painters for years, if every one of them had as many arms and hands as Vishnoo.'

In Gerace Lear witnessed a great local Festa, which he described with equal enjoyment and skill:

In the late afternoon we all repaired to the walls of the town to gaze at the procession of the saint's image, followed by the inmates of every one of the monasteries, and by all the ecclesiastics of the place. On the rocky platform, far below Gerace, yet elevated high above the maritime plain, are several convents, and far, far over the terraces of crags, among which they are built, the long line of the procession crept slowly, with attendant bands of music and firing of cannon – a curious scene, and not easy to portray. Hence, as evening was closing and the last golden streams of sunset had ceased to gild the merry scene, we came to the castle, where hundreds of peasants were dancing to the music of Zampognari; black-hooded women ranged in tiers on the rock terrace, sate like dark statues against the amber western sky; and gloomy and massive Norman ruins frowned over the misty gulf beneath with gloomier grandeur; the full moon rose high and formed a picturesque contrast with the Festa lights, which sparkled on the dark background of the pure heaven; and all combined to create one of those scenes which must ever live in the memory, and can only be formed in imagination, because neither painting nor description can do them justice.

Perhaps what impressed him most on this journey was the awesome mountain of Pentedatilo, on the way to Reggio:

Having gained the high ground opposite, the appearance of Pentedatilo is perfectly magical, and repays whatever trouble the effort to reach it may so far have cost. Wild spires of stone shoot up into the air, barren and clearly defined, in the form (as its name implies) of a gigantic hand against the sky, and in the crevices and holes of this fearfully savage pyramid the houses of Pentedatilo are wedged, while darkness and terror brood over all the abyss around this, the strangest of human abodes.

*Opposite:* Pentedatilo.

.Lear and his companions had for some time sensed that there was an atmosphere of tension among the places they travelled through and the people they met. He gives a very amusing account of their reception in Gioiosa by the local landowner and squire, Baron Rivettini, who appeared to be thrown into an extreme state of agitation by their appearance, and met all their questions and proposals with an endless repetition of *perche?* 'used in a breathless manner, on the slightest provocation'. Lear described his whole household as ill at ease, regarding their looks and movements 'with unabated watchfulness, as if we might explode, or escape through the ceiling at any unexpected moment'. They reached Reggio and crossed the Strait of Messina, and, leaving Proby in Sicily, Lear and Ciccio returned a few days later, when at last the mystery was explained. The first, premature explosions of the revolution of 1848 had overwhelmed the town. When they tried to get into their hotel and asked for their keys, a drunken waiter appeared, who cried out: 'There are no more keys – there are no more passports, no more kings, no more laws, no more judges, no more nothing! Nothing but love and liberty, friendship and the constitution! ai! o⁄o⁄o⁄o⁄o⁄orra birra bà!!'

Lear finally got back to Messina, where he and Proby decided to cut short their tour in Calabria and left by steamer for Naples. After about a week they resumed their travels, but in Basilicata and other territories of the Kingdom of Naples well away from the troubled

Bova: '. . . truly magnificent was the view, looking back from the points of rock where we frequently halted to rest, after passing the thick oak woods which encircle Bova'.

*Opposite:* Santa Maria di Polsi: '. . . one of the most remarkable scenes I ever beheld. . . . Here all around, above and below, is close wood and mountain – no outlet, no variety – stern solitude and the hermit sentiment reign supreme.'

75

Constantinople, watercolour,
September 1848.

provinces of Calabria. It was a hurried tour, lasting only until 4
October, and the Journal is correspondingly brief, though not without
its vivid and amusing moments.

The unremitting energy which Lear had shown throughout, his
determination to push on regardless of all discomforts and trials,
and in every new place to start sketching the moment he arrived, is
almost unbelievable; but new landscapes were for him an elixir and
tonic that never failed to key his capacities up to their highest pitch.
His companion does not seem to have been made of the same metal.
When he died ten years later, his sister believed he had never recovered
from the strain of his travels on this occasion.

It was on this expedition that Lear one evening overheard two
young Englishmen talking in the inn where they were lodging. 'I
say, Dick,' said one to the other, 'do you know who that fellow is
we were talking to last night?' 'No?' 'Why, he's nothing but a dirty
landscape-painter.' From that moment, Lear adopted the title for
himself of 'Dirty Landscape Painter' or 'Landskip Painter'.

The *Journals of a Landscape Painter in Albania and Illyria* was published
in 1851, and describes travels which he undertook between September and November 1848 and April and June 1849. The interval
between these and his Calabrian travels Lear spent partly in Malta,
partly packing up his things in Rome, which he had decided to leave
now for good and all, and partly in Corfu – his first visit to an island
which he came to think of almost as an earthly paradise. While in
Corfu he had the good fortune to meet the British Ambassador in
Turkey, Sir Stratford Canning, who was travelling back from London

Constantinople, watercolour, 1848.

to Constantinople with his family. Lear was already acquainted with them, and got on with them; now Lady Canning insisted that Lear should accompany them to Turkey. A golden opportunity for him, he immediately realized, and he agreed without hesitation. The party stopped for some time in Athens, where Lear met a friend called Charles Church, a good Greek scholar and linguist and nephew of Sir Richard Church, who had commanded Greek forces in the War of Independence. Together they decided to explore the Peloponnese, but the journey was ill-starred from the start. Lear was badly hurt by a fall from his horse, then fell seriously ill from an insect bite, and, after having been brought back to Athens, was too weak to go with the Cannings to Constantinople. When he did follow them he had another attack of fever, and it was only due to the ministrations of Lady Canning – 'as kind as 70 mothers' – that he recovered as completely as he did. Indomitably, after several weeks of eager sketching, he set out for Salonica, intending to join Charles Church again at Mount Athos. An outbreak of cholera, however, prevented him reaching either Mount Athos or Church. He therefore set out to travel westwards through Macedonia to Albania, with only a Bulgarian dragoman, Giorgio Kozzáchi, as companion. He was crossing what was still Turkey in Europe at that time, but was soon to become once more part of independent Greece. In between the two journeys, the crucial meeting with Franklin Lushington took place in Malta, and Lushington started off with him on the spring journey of 1849, though he had to leave by the end of April. By the time Lear was on his way back he had in effect, between September and June, covered the whole of the Greek peninsula. He was in the highest spirits, and on his return to England devoted himself to polishing the sketches he had made, preparing from them the lithograph illustrations for the book, and writing up the diary notes which were to form the basis of it.

*Journals of a Landscape Painter in Albania and Illyria* is not, perhaps, quite as lively or funny as the Calabrian book, and only a few of the illustrations have the sombre Romantic intensity of the plates in that book. Nevertheless it is uniquely Learean, full of fascinating incidents and glowing descriptions, and had a well-deserved success. Lear's sketching activities seemed extremely strange and suspicious to the natives of the more remote places he visited, and frequently he had to have a guard to protect him. Moments of anxiety were frequent, but he showed an astonishing determination, equanimity and sense of humour in the trickiest circumstances. On 26 September, for instance,

no sooner had I settled to draw – forgetful of Bekír the guard – than forth came the populace of Elbassán, one by one, and two by two, to a mighty host they grew, and there were soon from eighty to a hundred spectators collected, with earnest curiosity in every look; and when I had sketched such of the principal buildings as they could recognise, a universal shout of 'Shaitán!' burst from the crowd; and strange to relate, the greater part of the mob put their fingers into their mouths and whistled furiously, after the manner of butcher-boys in England. Whether this was a sort of spell against my magic I do not know; but the absurdity of sitting still on a rampart to make a drawing, while a great crowd of people whistled at me with all their might, struck me so forcibly, that come what might of it, I could not resist going off into convulsions of laughter, an impulse the Gheghes seemed to sympathise with, as one and all shrieked with delight, and the ramparts resounded with hilarious merriment. Alas! this was of no long duration, for one of those tiresome dervishes – in whom, with their green turbans, Elbassán is rich – soon came up, and yelled, 'Shaitán scroo! – Shaitán!' (the Devil draws! – the Devil!) in my ears with all his force; seizing my book also, with an awful frown, shutting it, and pointing to the sky, as intimating that heaven would not allow such impiety. It was vain after this to attempt more. . . .

One cannot help thinking that in this story one has the origin of one of Lear's favourite nonsense epithets, 'scroobious'.

He gives an equally amusing description of his encounter with Alí, the young Bey of the town of Króia perched on the top of its 'bare, craggy, dark mountain'. He relates how he was received by Alí,

a lad of eighteen or nineteen, dressed in the usual blue frock-coat now adopted by Turkish nobles or officers. A file of kilted and armed retainers were soon ordered to marshal me into a room where I was to sleep, and the little Bey seemed greatly pleased with the fun of doing hospitality to so novel a creature as a Frank. . . . After changing my dress, the Bey sent to say that supper should be served in an hour, he having eaten at sunset, and in the meantime he would be glad of my society; so I took my place on the sofa by the little gentleman's side, and Giorgio, sitting on the ground, acted as interpreter. . . . At length, when the conversation was flagging, he was moved to discourse about ships that went without sails, and coaches that were impelled without horses; and to please him I drew a steamboat and a railway carriage; on which he asked if they made any noise; and I replied by imitating both the inventions in question in the best manner I could think of – 'Tik⁄tok, tik⁄tok, tokka, tokka, tokka, tokka – tok' (crescendo), and 'squish⁄squash, squish⁄squash, squish⁄squash, thump⁄bump' – for the land and sea engines respectively – a noisy novelty, which so intensely delighted Alí Bey, that he fairly threw himself back on the divan, and laughed as I never saw Turk laugh before.

Of a very different character is Lear's description of his reception in the Akrokeraunian citadel of Khimára, the wildest place he visited in all his journeys. He was led to a house where

in a dark room of great size, a mat and cushions were spread for me, and there was no lack of company. . . . Circles of long⁄haired Khimáriotes thronged the floor. Many of these, both outside and inside the house, extended their hands for mine to shake, I supposed from being aware of Frank modes of salutation; but among them, three or four gave me so peculiar a twist or crack of my fingers, that I was struck by its singularity; though it was not until my hand had been held firmly for a repetition of this manoeuvre, accompanied by a look of interrogation from the holder, that the thought flashed on my mind, that what I observed was a concerted signal. I shortly became fully aware that I was among people, who, from some cause or other, had fled from justice in other lands.

Of these was one who, with his face entirely muffled excepting one eye, kept aloof in the darker part of the chamber, until having thoroughly scrutinized me, he came forward, and dropping his capote, discovered to my horror and amazement, features which, though disfigured by an enormous growth of hair, I could not fail to recognize. 'The world is my city now,' said he; 'I am become a savage like them with whom I dwell. What is life to me?' And covering his face again, he wept with a heart⁄breaking bitterness only life⁄exiles can know.

Lear gives no explanation of this mysterious encounter – indeed it would have been a breach of trust if he had – and no one to my know⁄ledge has ever provided any plausible clue to identify the tragic exile of Khimára.

A few days later he reached Tepeléni, the former stronghold of Alí Pasha, famous rebel against the Porte and splendour⁄loving despot, who combined ruthless cruelty with cunning diplomacy and an exceptional degree of administrative skill in the territories of which he had made himself master. When at the height of his power, in 1809, he had entertained Byron, who described his visit in a long letter to his mother, and afterwards in a well⁄known passage of *Childe Harold*. Now all was ruin and desolation, inspiring melancholy thoughts in Lear as he picked his way among the crumbling walls and deserted chambers. He wrote that, of all the scenes he had visited, 'the palace of Alí Pasha at Tepeléni will continue most vividly printed on my recollection'.

Sketch of a Greek or an Albanian mending a rug, attributed to Edward Lear.

*Overleaf: page 80*, the Gorge of Tempe: 'Well might the ancients extol this grand defile'; *page 81*, Berát: 'Beyond the bazaars, which are extensive and well filled, is a wide open space by the river, whence the view of the dark gorge of the Beratíno, the town and castle are truly wondrous.'

Berat
October 1848.

132

81

In the villages, he stayed mostly at the local 'khans', which he described as 'a species of public-house rented by the keeper or Khanji from the Government', open to all comers. The accommodation he found in these inns was no more luxurious or reposeful than he had found in the wilder parts of Calabria, as his serio-comic invocation of them indicates:

Midnight, O khans of Albania! Alas! the night is not yet worn through! I lie, barricaded by boxes and bundles from the vicinity of the stable, and enduring with patience the fierce attacks of numberless fleas. All the khan sleeps, save two cats, which indulge in festive bouncings, and save a sleepless donkey, which rolls too contiguously to my head. The wood-fire, blazing up, throws red gleams on discoloured arches within whose far gloom the eye catches the form of sleeping Albanian groups. Bulky spiders, allured by the warmth, fall thick and frequent from the raftered ceiling. All is still, except the horses champing straw within, and the gurgle of the rapid river chafing without.

It was after reading this book that Tennyson wrote his lines 'To E.L. on his Travels in Greece':

Monastir (now in Yugoslavia, called Bitola): oil painting of unknown date, but obviously based on drawings done on Lear's Albanian tour.

*Athos — all things fair.*

*to E. L. on his travels in Greece.)*

*Monastery of Simopetra. Mount Athos.*

Illyrian woodlands, echoing falls
Of water, sheets of summer glass,
The long divine Peneian pass,
The vast Akrokeraunian walls,

Tomohrit, Athos, all things fair,
With such a pencil, such a pen,
You shadow forth to distant men,
I read and felt that I was there:

And trust me while I turn'd the page,
And track'd you still on classic ground,
I grew in gladness till I found
My spirits in the golden age.

For me the torrent ever pour'd
And glisten'd – here and there alone
The broad-limbed gods at random thrown
By fountain-urns; – and Naiads oar'd

A glimmering shoulder under gloom
Of cavern pillars; on the swell
The silver lily heav'd and fell;
And many a slope was rich in bloom

From him that on the mountain lea
By dancing rivulets fed his flocks,
To him who sat upon the rocks,
And fluted to the morning sea.

Monastery of Simopetra, Mount Athos: one of a number of drawings executed about 1880, towards the end of Lear's life, for Tennyson's poem 'To E. L. on his Travels in Greece'.

After the Calabrian and Albanian Journals, Lear did not publish any more travel books for nearly twenty years. He had kept full diaries of his travels in Egypt, Crete, and elsewhere, but they never

The Forest of Bavella, Corsica, in an original drawing of 1868.

saw the light, though in January 1868 he wrote to Lady Waldegrave: 'At present I am not drawing at all nor painting – but writing: the rough copy of my Cretan journals is done, and nearly that of the Nile 1854: the Nubia of 1867 will follow, and I mean to get all three ready for publication with illustrations, if possible next summer, whether in parts or volumes I can't yet say. By degrees I want to topographize all the journeyings of my life. . . .' In the late summer of 1868, however, inspired partly by a new friendship which he had started at Cannes with the French novelist Prosper Mérimée, author of the famous story of Corsican vendetta *Colomba*, he decided to make a tour of the island. *The Journal of a Landscape Painter in Corsica*, the third and last of the Journals to appear during his lifetime, was published early in 1870. It was dedicated to Franklin Lushington.

On this tour Lear decided to hire a two-horse carriage instead of travelling on foot or on horseback: partly, it seems, because he felt himself no longer equal, in so mountainous an island, to the great exertions of his earlier travels, partly because he wanted to complete it within a rather tight schedule of time – after the snow had cleared and before the oppressive heat of summer started. With Giorgio Cocali to look after him, he left at the beginning of April, and was back in Cannes at the beginning of June, with over three hundred drawings made in sixty days.

At the start of the tour he met a formidable English lady, Miss Campbell, of that all but extinct race of indomitable and eccentric female English travellers. Lear described her as 'a vast and man-like maiden who roars and raves about Corsica'. She gave him a great deal of useful information, and also warned him against the coach-man he had engaged. Unfortunately, Lear did not heed her warning, and was involved in a terrible accident on one of the mountain roads. The coachman, in spite of Lear's protests, had taken to ill-treating the horses, and on this occasion he beat them so savagely about the head that they backed to the edge of the precipice and stumbled over with carriage, driver and all, though luckily not with Lear or Giorgio as they were walking at the time. One horse was killed, the carriage smashed to pieces. Lear returned to Ajaccio, badly shaken by the horror of it, but hired a new carriage a few days later with a new coachman, a young man by the name of Domenico who was a great success. Domenico brought with him 'a small spotty dog of amiable and watchful deportment, called Flora', who trotted on ahead everywhere. This was probably the only dog Lear ever took to. At the end of the tour, he wrote: 'Flora and Company are dis-missed with esteem. . . . Farewell, spotty little beast of excellent qualities – Flora, best of dogs!'

During his two months Lear managed to explore the whole

One of the engravings of the Forest of Bavella as it appeared in *Journal of a Landscape Painter in Corsica*, 1870: 'At times the mist is suddenly lifted like a veil, and discloses the whole forest – as it were in the pit of an immense theatre confined between towering rock-walls, and filling up with its thousands of pines all the great hollow. . . .'

island, in a series of criss-crossing journeys. Even if the *Journal of a Landscape Painter in Corsica* lacks the sparkle of the two previous Journals, it shows that his appetite for the beauties of landscape was undiminished. His delight in Corsican nature is revealed all through; repeatedly he records his wonder at the great forests of pine trees, the woods of oak and ilex, the evergreen maquis and the carpets of wild flowers, the cistus and cyclamen above all. He is struck again and again by the 'awfully mysterious' and 'exquisitely beautiful' mountain scenery – qualities which come out in the best of his drawings, though much is lost in the wood-engravings which he was obliged to have made, instead of lithographs, for the illustrations. The pass of Bavella impressed him most deeply, but the forests of Valdoniello and Aitone came very close. Of the last-named he wrote:

All the way up the pass numberless charms arrest your attention – the sunlight twinkling and glittering through the young yellow leaves of the great beech trees, or glancing on their tall silvery stems, here black with moss, there with long floating tresses of pale green lichen waving from their branches. You look up to the highest summits above the pass, where masses of pine contrast darkly with cushions of gold-green beechwood; lingering in shady hollows you mark the chequered lights on the road, or on the pure white snow, which higher up is lying in wreaths along the banks by the wayside. Nowhere is there any lack of the beautiful throughout.

Bastia: '. . . there is not much to be got out of Bastia in a picturesque sense'. From *Journal of a Landscape Painter in Corsica*, 1870.

A little later on, he makes an interesting observation about the origin of his enthusiasm for landscape. 'At 4 p.m., always descending, I reached the cleared level space in which stands the principal establishment of M. Chauton – a busy little world, in great contrast with the scenery around it, and reminding me of Robinson Crusoe's settlement as represented in beautiful Stothard drawings, those exquisite creations of landscape which first made me, when a child, long to see similar realities.'

Lear embellished not only his letters, and many pages of his diaries, with quick little sketches and comic doodles, but also on occasion his personal copies of his own travel books. The Corsican Journal is an amusing example: on the verso of the title page there are several ink blots which he has transformed into sketches of a guardsman and a man with mustachios. 'Two blots on Corsica! O dear, dear, dear, Mr Edward Lear,' he scribbled above, together with a caricature of his cat, adding the words: 'Foss did it!'

View near Calvi, pen and watercolour, 30 May 1868: '. . . still the eye delights in fresh and enchanting views'.

Sparta, pen and watercolour, 2.30–3 p.m., 23 March 1849. This is a typical example of Lear's working method, with such notes to himself as 'abominable red-roofed white houses – put them in shadow' (no. 12, half-way up at the left); 'immense plain of foliage' (no. 100, behind the houses); 'torrents running down XXX' (at the foot of the mountains).

65.

Pyramid with the Sphinx and palms, pen and watercolour, Cairo, 21 March 1858.

As I have already mentioned, Lear's decision to devote his career to landscape painting was taken very early on in his life, after his increasingly weak eyesight made the meticulously detailed bird and animal drawing, by which he had originally made a name, impossible to go on with. During his tours in the Lake District and in Ireland, in 1834 and 1835, the love of landscape, which the Stothard drawings had helped to inspire in him, resulted in his discovery that he had a gift for recording in line and colour wash what had so pleased his eye. He was always extremely independent, and of a restless, roving disposition, and he judged, accurately, that he could make a living, if only a modest one, by exploiting this gift.

There is no doubt that he thought it would be by producing highly finished oil paintings out of the sketches, the rapid notations he made on his travels, that his reputation would be secured. He laboured at them with endless patience and care; he went to school with the Pre-Raphaelites to improve his technical competence; he exhibited them throughout his life, and from time to time managed to persuade patrons to buy them, for sums which, though they may appear less than handsome today, were, in terms of Victorian purchasing power, reasonably rewarding. Some of them are now in public galleries, some in private collections, where they would hang scarcely noticed today were it not for the steadily increasing admiration for what Lear himself estimated to be of far less worth, the original coloured drawings themselves.

His industry on his travels was such that he made enormous quantities of sketches, often five or six a day when the light was right. On his arrival at a new place in the evening, he would decide on the most suitable spots from which to draw, and be up the next morning at dawn to start work. In the middle of the day, as he travelled onwards, he would descend from carriage or horseback the moment he spied some especially favourable vantage point, some ideally picturesque view. On these sketches he would make notes about colour or light or conformation of the land, and elaborate them in the evening, or later on at the end of a tour. He would, as he called it, 'pen them out', sometimes making several copies, and brush colour or tonal washes over these drawings.

He sold the watercolours for very little indeed when he exhibited them, in his own rooms in Rome, in London, in Malta or Corfu, or later on at Cannes or San Remo. People bought them because they were pleased to have attractive records of places they knew, or would like to have known. But selling them was hard and often exasperating work. Visitors, particularly women in local society, would come to his exhibitions as if to a tea-party, chatter gaily and vapidly, waste his time, and depart without having bought anything. In 1866, after his stay in Malta, he wrote wryly to Lady Waldegrave: 'My whole winter gains – twenty-five pounds – must remain a melanchollical reminiscence of the rocky island and its swell community.' Then commissions would all of a sudden arrive for a

Suli, the ancestral home of Giorgio Cocali, pen and watercolour, 6 May 1849.

Detail of tortoises, plants, etc. from a watercolour of Parnassus, 2.00 p.m., 12 April 1849.

*Opposite:* Detail from an oil painting of unknown date of the Temple of Apollo at Bassae.

batch of watercolours, and he would be happy as well as busy for a while. In spite of these intervals of good fortune, the struggle never seemed to come to an end. Towards the end of his life he wrote to Fortescue: 'Old friends cannot go on always buying, but I have always to go on eating.'

The rise of his reputation as a watercolourist makes an extra-ordinary story. The first stirring of interest after his death began when Lady Strachey published two volumes of his letters, in 1907 and 1911, which revealed to a wider public what a unique and delightful letter-writer he was, and what a fascinating personality. By the time the second volume came out, the first had gone through four editions. Then came a pause. Most of his work was still in private hands. Suddenly, in 1929, at a series of auction sales in London, a large number of his drawings appeared, as well as his personal diaries and manuscripts, all of which had been left by Lear to Franklin Lushington and were being sold by his daughters. This was followed, a few months later, by a sale at Sotheby's in which part of Lord Northbrook's collection of Leareana came on to the market. New York collectors began to be interested, and the greater part of these collections eventually found its way across the Atlantic.

Nevertheless, the critics and the dealers in England were still not particularly interested. The poet William Plomer, who early on in his career became an enthusiast for Lear's work as draughtsman and painter, remembered picking up examples of his work in various print shops in and around London, during the twenties and thirties, for a few shillings, or at the most a pound or two. It was not until Angus Davidson's sympathetic and deeply perceptive biographical study appeared in 1938 that Lear's watercolours began to be taken seriously and his achievement to be appreciated at its true worth. Since then, his work as an artist – as one facet of a many-sided genius – has risen strongly in public estimation and value. The Gennadius Library in Athens, for instance, acquired an assortment of his Greek watercolours in 1929 for £25. There were 192 separate items: they could scarcely be worth less than £25,000 at today's prices. By far the greater part of the watercolours and sketches which were acquired by American collectors, notably Osgood Field and Philip Hofer, have gone to the Houghton Library at Harvard, where they are housed with the thirty-five volumes of his personal diaries. This is now without rival the greatest depository of Leareana in the world, and, with its basic collection of nearly 3,500 sketches and water-colours, is of almost incalculable value.

It was about the middle of the eighteenth century that English artists were beginning to be fired by an enthusiasm to travel abroad, to France, Germany, Italy (above all to Rome) and even further into

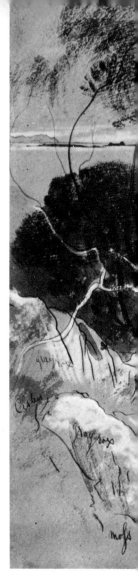

Within the image (handwritten annotations): *blue sea*, *green*, *& castles*, *(25)*, *From below Spartilla, Corfu, 9.10 a.m. 21 April 1866.*

the lands of the eastern Mediterranean, bringing back sketchbooks and portfolios filled with coloured drawings of all the places they had visited, ancient ruins, mountainous and exotic scenery and cities on the 'Grand Tour' routes, thus feeding an appetite that had grown steadily among the educated classes at home. The first thirty-five years of the nineteenth century have been called 'the Golden Age of English Water-Colour'; Girtin had died as a young man in 1802, but during this period Bonington, Cotman, Prout and, greatest of all, Turner were all at work on the Continent. More contemporary with Lear were such artists as Boys, Danby and Roberts. In fact Lear was one of a large company of English artists of his time dedicated to their profession as 'topographical landscape painters'. He is not the greatest

*Above:* Corfu, pen and watercolour, 9.00–10.00 a.m., 21 April 1866.

*Opposite above:* Lefkhimni, pen and watercolour, 10 May 1862.

*Opposite below:* Potamos, pen and watercolour, 8 and 23 April and 3.00 p.m., 28 January

Athens, pen and watercolour, 5.00
p.m., 8 April 1849.

of them, but no one of them, with the possible exception of Turner,
gives the same impression of feeling his way towards an approach to
the drawing of landscape that has come to be thought of as essentially
modern. He had an altogether exceptional gift for bold simplification
of line – a gift that comes out equally strongly in his nonsense drawings – and for creating mood by the simplest of means. He once wrote
to Hunt: 'I cannot but know that there is a vein of poetry within me
that *ought to have* come out – though I begin to doubt if it ever will.'
Even leaving aside his actual nonsense songs and the strongly poetic
descriptions that abound in his travel books and letters, most modern
admirers of his work would, I think, disagree with this self-estimate.
Lear was lucky enough to be working at a time when the classical
lands had still not been 'tidied up', nor excavated so extensively with
meticulous scientific care, nor built over in concrete agglomerations of
sprawling suburbs. His drawings of Athens, when it was still little
more than an overgrown village clustered round the ruins of the
Acropolis, of the great mound of Mycenae before Schliemann, and
of many other still virgin sites in the Greece he loved so deeply, show
the most sensitive poetic response to the wildness of nature proliferating
through centuries that had all but obliterated the grandeur of past
civilization. Almost all the drawings, for instance, that he brought
back from his tour of Crete in 1864, in the middle of his finest period
of maturity, are deeply imbued with poetic feeling, with a Turneresque
suggestion of mood in air and cloud. The drawing is wonderfully
uninhibited and expressive, with a fresh, spirited but remarkably
sensitive line; distance is conveyed with a subtle understanding of
receding space, and yet the furthest mountains give that accurate
impression of solidity which made one of his more scientific admirers

exclaim that he could always recognize the geological formation of a landscape from Lear's painting of it. When he included buildings and towns he would sometimes draw them with a broad simplification of outline, sometimes with a minutely detailed appreciation of their structure without disturbing the harmony of the whole. At the bottom of his sketches, as Holman Hunt noted, he would scribble joking annotations for his later 'penning out' or the more elaborate oil compositions that evolved from them: 'rox' – 'lams' – 'Time and assfuddle' (for thyme and asphodel) – 'Owl! Pipe! Pipe! Pipe!' – 'Tortoises!!' (with a little sketch of a tortoise beside it). As Sir Osbert Lancaster has written, 'the careful recording vision that had made him so superlative an illustrator of natural history books, allied with that rapid calligraphic execution which gives to his comic drawings their eternal freshness, render the best of his sketches records of the Greek countryside which have never been surpassed'.

Mycenae, pen and watercolour, 7.00 a.m., 31 March 1849.

*Above:* Delphi, pen and watercolour,
6.45 p.m., 16 April 1849.

*Opposite above:* Suda Bay, pen and
watercolour, 5 a.m., 24 May 1864.

*Opposite below:* Aptera, Crete, pen
and watercolour, 7.00 a.m., 4 May
1864.

*View in Villa Emily. Sanremo.*

*Above:* Villa Emily, Lear's first home in San Remo, as it is today.

*Above right:* Lear with Foss, from a letter written to Emily Tennyson, 5 January 1876.

In March 1871 Lear moved into the house he had built for himself on the plot of land he had chosen in San Remo, calling it the Villa Emily. He had a large painting room – and a garden, which he had never had before. Giorgio was there to look after him, and soon after he had settled in he acquired his famous cat, Foss, who appears in so many of the drawings with which he decorated his letters in the last phase of his life.

He wanted to make the Villa Emily his home for good. He had come back from his tour of Corsica in December 1868, and after a life of wandering he felt that the time had come for repose and ease, particularly as, in addition to his other ailments, he was now suffering from heart trouble. It was not to be. He had always dreamed of visiting India and Ceylon, and suddenly the opportunity arose. His friend Lord Northbrook, whose young cousin and secretary, Evelyn Baring, had been so close to him during his Corfu days, had been appointed Viceroy of India. He now wrote, suggesting that Lear should go with him: he would send him back, free of expense, after a year, and only asked as recompense that Lear should paint some pictures of India for him. After much heart-searching – always having been an extremely independent person he shrank from the idea of being caught up in the Viceregal suite and in Viceregal solemnities when he arrived in India – he decided to take the chance, set forth, but only got as far as Suez, where he found all the boats full; the only berth he could find, on a French boat, he missed by bad luck. Back he went to San Remo.

Nevertheless, he decided to try again the following year; and this time, with Giorgio at his side, he succeeded in sailing from Genoa, in the autumn of 1873, with a large number of commissions for Indian pictures in addition to Lord Northbrook's. He arrived in Bombay twenty-seven days later, on 22 November.

Lear's *Indian Journal* was not published during his lifetime, and in fact was only edited (by Ray Murphy) for publication in 1953. It reveals that his response to new, strange scenes was as immediate and vivid as ever. 'Violent and amazing delight at the wonderful varieties of life and dress here,' he noted as soon as he disembarked. 'O fruits! O flowers! O queer vegetables!' In spite of such characteristic outbursts of pleasure at what he was seeing, the Journal makes it clear that the expedition, with the enormously long journeys he made all over the country, mainly by train, and the changes of climate they involved from the torrid plains to the cool of the mountain valleys, was an experience that tested his endurance severely. He was bewildered and exasperated during his first few days in India, and throughout his visit displayed irritation, fussiness and short temper, often vent-

Lord Northbrook, Viceroy of India (seated in the centre of the group), with his cousin and Private Secretary Evelyn Baring on his left, from a photograph taken *c.* 1873.

ing his ill-humour on the ever loyal Giorgio – though immediately afterwards recording appreciation, affection and regret. Bouts of ill-health plagued him, and he had trouble with his right eye. Again and again he thought of packing up and going home. He was maddened by the unreliability of Indian officials and servants, and by the frequent inadequacy of his lodgings; on earlier expeditions such trials would probably have been passed off in a couple of humorous paragraphs. Whenever he was the guest of high English administrators, he was distracted by the hubbub of their households. Government House at Calcutta he dubbed 'Hustlefussabad', in spite of the constant attentions of Northbrook and his cousin. Again and again he notes that he was 'cross, unwell, and wretched'. One curious feature of the Journal is that he records in detail what he drank – mostly beer, soda water and sherry, with an occasional 'peg' (presumably brandy) – and also what he ate every day. He was certainly not abstemious.

Roorkee, pen and watercolour, 2.00–5.00 p.m., 20 March 1874.

Agra, the Taj Mahal, pen and watercolour, 1874.

In spite of the many discomforts and misfortunes, he found much to enjoy, and not only in the constantly changing scenery and the colourful life of the people. He loved the 'comfort and quiet' of the dak bungalows in the mountains, 'far and by far the happiest Indian reposes'. He was in ecstasies over the splendour of the Taj Mahal, and wrote: 'Henceforth, let the inhabitants of the world be divided into two classes – them as has seen the Taj Mahal; and them as hasn't.' As was his wont, he made a number of friends among the kindly English officials who were his hosts. At Roorkee, he was immensely pleased to find that Major and Mrs Lang had three 'darling little girls, who all knew the Book of Nonsense, and to whom I sang "The Owl and the Pussy-cat"'. And in Allahabad, while he was drawing an owl for the landlord's little girl, another little girl who was watching cried out: 'O please draw a pussy-cat too!' He was delighted

Giorgio and Lear on an elephant, from a letter written by Lear to Lady Waldegrave, 25 October 1875.

to discover that the whole school knew his poem. All the time he was writing an immense number of letters to his friends, often very long, and completing an immense quantity of drawings: by the time he reached Poona in June he had made 560, as well as filling nine small sketchbooks.

He finished his expedition with a visit to Ceylon; but by then he was too exhausted to appreciate anything any more. He called the island 'a bore of the first quality'. The worst disasters of the whole adventure now overtook him. Giorgio fell ill with dysentery, and Lear, already suffering from a bad throat, had to devote most of his time to nursing him. When he strained his back and developed lumbago, he decided that enough was enough, cut the tour short, made his way back to Bombay and sailed for Europe.

Poona, watercolour, 3.00–4.00 p.m., 15 June 1874.

*Opposite:* Kinchinjunga, near Darjeeling, oil painting, 1873–4.

Pension Major. Serrabassa.

~~Italia~~    Abetone

Pistojese.

August 18. 1883.

My dear Mrs Tennyson,

I meant to have written to you directly
after I got your letter of the 14th — which came up
here — by reason of the delay from its going round
by Mendrisio, only on the 18th. But I have not been up
to writing, having been quite knocked up — first
by my troubles at Mte Generoso, & then by the great
heat at ~~Milano~~ & Bologna, — & by the jolting journey
to this mountain place, where nevertheless I am
slowly getting better through good air & comparative
quiet.        Your very kind letter was most
delightful to me, & I do not know any one who
could write such: & all you write is most
valuable & helpful. But since my dear good
George's leaving me, nothing has afforded me
so much comfort as these lines,

"I held it truth with him who sing
" To one clear harp in divers tones,
" That men may rise on stepping stones
" Of their dead selves to higher things."

It is well for foolish people to say, — how can
a mere servant be such a stepping stone? — but

Back home in San Remo, Lear cherished the hope that he could begin to enjoy a peaceful evening to his life. Instead, the next few years were crowded with painful disappointments, constant illness, and many deaths among his friends and relations. To start with, he found that the Villa Emily had been broken into and burgled during his absence. Very little in fact had been stolen, according to Hubert Congreve; but the state of confusion and violation in which he found all his belongings was a deep shock to him. More permanently distressing was the steady decline in health of his old servant and companion Giorgio, who had never fully recovered from the dysentery he caught in Ceylon, and who now heard that his wife, his mother and his brothers in Corfu had all died. He was deeply shaken, and begged to be allowed to go back to the island. Lear sent for his son Lambi to take him home, and with the aid of Hubert accompanied him as far as Brindisi. Nevertheless, Giorgio did make at least a partial recovery, as Lear found when he stopped at Corfu on his return from his last visit to England in the summer. He took him to Monte Generoso, above Lake Como – where he himself was to spend many summers from that time on – and when his strength was equal to the journey brought him back with Lambi to San Remo. All seemed well; Lear's spirits revived; he was working at his paintings, writing more nonsense poems and enjoying his garden, and felt immensely refreshed by a visit from Lushington and his family. But Giorgio's recovery did not last for long. He was saddened by the moral collapse of Lambi, who had been stealing and getting into debt, and had in the end to be sent back to Corfu. This was followed by a breakdown, when Giorgio lost his memory, disappeared, and was eventually found in a completely dazed state in the hills above Toulon. He died in 1883: in a letter to Emily Tennyson, Lear wrote of his 'constant fidelity, activity, humility, goodness of disposition, endless cheerfulness, honesty, patience and untold other virtues'. Following the dismissal of Lambi, Giorgio's other two sons, Nicola and Demetrio, had come to San Remo to look after their father and help Lear; but after Giorgio's death Nicola began to waste away with tuberculosis, and Demetrio went the way of Lambi. He too had to be sent back to Corfu. Lear had hoped much from the boys, believing that they might grow up to be a living memory of Giorgio and as such the solace of his old age. The extinction of this hope added to the melancholy of his final years.

Before Giorgio's death, what seemed at the time would be the greatest blow of all to Lear's anticipation of a reasonably contented old age was his discovery of the scheme to build a new five-storey hotel at the bottom of his garden. All his plans, he felt, were utterly in ruins; but as so often before in his life, his well-to-do friends came

A photograph on glass of Emily Tennyson.

*Opposite:* Letter to Emily Tennyson from Lear, 18 August 1883, mentioning Giorgio's death and quoting (incorrectly) from 'In Memoriam'.

A present-day photograph showing the hotel that blocked Lear's view from the Villa Emily. He wrote in October 1878: 'A huge hotel is to be built just below my garden: if it is on the left side it will shut out all my sea view; a calamity as afflicts me.'

*Opposite:* Letter to Hallam Tennyson from Lear, 16 September 1880, complaining about the new hotel: 'I meant to have written to you from the Shaws of the Muddy Tooranian Sea, – but when I got to Sanremo . . . I found that it was quite impossible to use my painting room owing to the immense glare & reflex of the 5 storey high Hotel. . . . Until the sun gets farther round – i.e. about mid October – all my rooms are useless for painting. . . . Certainly, a more devilish injury was never inflicted by 2 English people & a Gerwoman on any unoffending artist.'

to his rescue. After the death of his beloved wife, the former Lady Waldegrave, in 1879, Chichester Fortescue, who had been created Lord Carlingford a few years before, came out to San Remo to visit Lear. He was able to persuade him to buy another piece of land nearby and build another villa, as like the Villa Emily as possible. Finance was the problem, as Lear's own resources, at least until the Villa Emily was sold, were in no way adequate. Lord Northbrook lent him £2,000, and further sums were contributed by other friends, including Lord Derby and Fortescue himself – a further proof of the loyalty that Lear had always inspired in his friends, even though, in the cases of Fortescue and Lushington, their affection was far from equal to Lear's love for them.

The Villa Emily took a long time to sell, and Lear, finding that even with these generous loans from his friends he needed more money, decided to sell off a great mass of drawings still in his possession by an exhibition in London. Sorting them out seems to have been a painful process – he felt he was saying goodbye to the most adventurous and zestful part of his life. Meanwhile the Villa Tennyson was at last finished, and he moved in with Foss. He started his 'Wednesdays' again, but became more and more bored with the business of attending to the visitors who might (and generally did not) buy his paintings. His thoughts turned frequently, as his strength began to ebb, to death. He wrote to Fortescue from his new home:

I find written in my diary for some days past, 'Be thankful for good sleep and better health', and it is a pleasant fact that I am certainly much better than I was a year ago, having only had one baddish fit of fainting and giddiness latterly, and feeling generally stronger. This however by no means shuts my eyes to the fact that I am

Grand Hotel. Varése.

Varése. Lombardia.
Sept. 16. 1880

My dear Hallam,

I meant to have written to you from the
Shaws of the Muddy Tooranian Sea,— but when
I got to Sanremo, (August 28) I found that it was
quite impossible to use my painting room owing
to the immense glare & reflex of the 5 storey high
hotel built by dirty Janet Shuttleworth. Until the
sun gets farther round,— ie — about mid October,—
all my rooms are useless for painting, & even then
only those I have gone to the expense of putting new
windows to are available. Certainly, a more
devilish injury was never inflicted by 2 English
people & a Scotswoman on any unoffending artist.
So I came up here, with some convenient work
for Ld Derby & Sir J. Lubbock, besides 2 of the 200
A illustrations; &c,— unless I go for a lark to
Monte Generoso,— here I shall remain till about
October the 6th,— when I shall return to my poor dear
miserably spoiled house for the winter.

Now the origin of the name, "Muddy Tooranian
Sea is this. When I left Stratford Place, there
was a big picture of mine, "Masada, on the Dead
Sea";— (now Lady Lyttelton's,) being taken down with
all the rest by workmen. On which, a boy said,
"Vy is it called the Dead sea?"— whereto replied
an older one — "You stoopid! do you think
the name of a sea or a Hottentot has anythink
to do with its' natur? Vy, ven I vos a
sailor & went all over the vorld, I vos in
the White sea, as vornt White at all.—
nor the Red sea vornt Red, nor the Black Sea
Black, nor the Muddy Tooranian Sea,
as vornt Muddy nohow, but, quite
contrairy— all blue!" (Stoopid boy

The Villa Tennyson, Lear's final home in San Remo, under construction. He wrote in April 1881: 'The new villa Tennyson is nearly done, and the old flower-supporting arches are all removed hence and put up there. 8 men is a digging and manuring all day – and costs 16s. a week.'

one whole year nearer to the end – whatever and whenever that may be; and there were times some months ago when I believed it to be close at hand. I cannot say I find any terrors in the contemplation of death; I have lived to ascertain positively that much of the evil of my life has arisen from congenital circumstances over which I – as a child – could have had no control; a good deal too has been the result of various ins and outs of life vagaries, and what is called chance – which chance I don't believe in, for if I did I must give up all idea of a God at all. I know also that I owe an immensity to the assistance of friends, – and neither do I put that down to chance. So, on the whole, I am tolerably placid and Abercrombical, compared with what I used to be.

Two events in particular cheered him at this time. While he was staying at Monte Generoso, Queen Victoria's daughter, the Princess Royal, and her husband, the future and so briefly reigning Emperor of Germany, arrived; to his delight, they remembered Lear from the days when he gave the Queen drawing lessons, and went for a walk with him. Lear described her as 'the most absolute duck of a Princess imaginable, so natural and unaffected, with a real simplicity one feels is not an affectation of simplicity'. It is said that the Queen herself, who was staying at Mentone, wanted to visit her old teacher and see his paintings, but abandoned the idea owing to the protocol complications involved in crossing the Italian frontier even so short a distance and for so short a visit.

The Villa Tennyson completed.

The other event was the news that Ruskin, in the *Pall Mall Magazine* of February 1886, had written: 'Surely the most beneficent and innocent of all books yet produced is the *Book of Nonsense*, with its corollary carols – inimitable and refreshing, and perfect in rhythm. I really don't know any author to whom I am half so grateful, for my idle self, as Edward Lear. I shall put him first of my hundred authors.' This praise from a man who was still regarded as the foremost critic in England was deeply satisfying to Lear who, much more perhaps than he was apt to admit, wanted to be recognized as a highly original nonsense-writer at a time when a just appreciation of his painting was still withheld, and a sense of failure haunted him. He immediately sent Ruskin a copy of the last nonsense poem he was ever to write, a poem so poignantly full of references to his own life – as it were dream transformations only partly concealed beneath the humorous surface – that it can scarcely be called nonsense:

> *O my agèd Uncle Arly!*
> *Sitting on a heap of Barley*
>   *Thro' the silent hours of night, –*
> *Close beside a leafy thicket : –*
> *On his nose there was a Cricket, –*
> *In his hat a Railway-Ticket ; –*
>   *(But his shoes were far too tight.)*

Lear and Foss, from a letter to
Hallam Tennyson, 16 June 1884.

Long ago, in youth, he squander'd
All his goods away, and wander'd
    To the Tiniskoop-hills afar.
There on golden sunsets blazing,
Every evening found him gazing, –
Singing, – 'Orb, you're quite amazing!
    How I wonder what you are!'

Like the ancient Medes and Persians,
Always by his own exertions
    He subsisted on those hills; –
Whiles, – by teaching children spelling, –
Or at times by merely yelling, –
Or at intervals by selling
    Propter's Nicodemus Pills.

Later, in his morning rambles
He perceived the moving brambles –
    Something square and white disclose; –
'Twas a First-class Railway-Ticket;
But, on stooping down to pick it
Off the ground, – a pea-green Cricket
    Settled on my uncle's Nose.

Never – never more, – oh! never,
Did that Cricket leave him ever, –
    Dawn or evening, day or night; –
Clinging as a constant treasure, –
Chirping with a cheerious measure, –
Wholly to my uncle's pleasure, –
    (Though his shoes were far too tight.)

So for three -and-forty winters
Till his shoes were worn to splinters,
    All those hills he wander'd o'er, –
Sometimes silent; – sometimes yelling; –
Till he came to Borley-Melling,
Near his old ancestral dwelling; –
    (But his shoes were far too tight.)

On a little heap of Barley
Died my agèd uncle Arly,
    And they buried him one night; –
Close beside the leafy thicket; –
There, – his hat and Railway-Ticket; –
There, – his ever-faithful Cricket; –
    (But his shoes were far too tight.)

Lear's last years were further saddened by family deaths. Of those brothers and sisters who survived childhood or youth in his exceptionally large family, many had emigrated to distant parts of the world, synonymous in his imaginings perhaps with the Hills of the Chankly Bore and the Coast of Coromandel. His brothers Henry and Frederick had left early on for the United States, and were the fathers of large families. Their lives were full of difficulties, and they made constant appeals to Edward and his sisters in England for help; during the American Civil War, Frederick's son was with the Confederate Army, Henry's four sons with the Union forces. Sarah married Charles Street, and after his death went out to New Zealand with her son Charles and her daughter Emily, who became Mrs Gillies and after whom, it is thought (not after Lady Tennyson) the Villa Emily was named. Sarah died while Lear was on his Indian expedition. At one moment he thought of sailing for New Zealand himself and living with her son Charles. Then the news came of Charles's sudden death, which deeply affected him. Mary and her husband Richard Boswell had followed Sarah to New Zealand, but Mary died at sea as she was returning to England after the failure of their enterprises. Eleanor, like Ann, remained in England, and married a prosperous banker, William Newson. Every two weeks, until she became totally blind, she and Lear exchanged letters with one another; when she died in 1885, Lear wrote that 'a sort of continuity of relationship seems now to be all at once mysteriously dissolved'.

Ann, Eleanor, Sarah and Mary were now all dead. In September 1887 the beloved cat Foss died, at the ripe old age of seventeen. In a life which provided so few outlets for the great fund of intimate affection which Lear had always felt within him, the death of this companion, who appears as his faithful follower in so many of the self-caricaturing drawings of the last phase of his life, was a hard blow of fate.

Scarcely less distressing than all these personal losses was his failure to complete and give to the world his so long cherished project of an edition of Tennyson's poems with his own illustrations. It seems likely that, after his troubles with the reproductions of his illustrations to the travel journals, he had become capricious and prickly about the technical problems. 'I go on irregularly at the A.T. illustrations,' he wrote, 'seeking a method of doing them by which I can eventually multiply my noo designs by photograph or autograph or sneezigraph or any other graph.' He had commissioned a young artist called Underhill to lithograph his drawings; he came to stay at the Villa in 1885 for two or three weeks, but though there were endless discussions, no satisfactory result came of it. Lushington came for a visit in November 1886, and wrote to Hallam Tennyson:

QUI SOTTO
STA SEPOLTO
IL MIO BUON
GATTO FOSS
ERA IN CASA MIA
30 ANNI E MORI
IL 26 7<sup>re</sup> 1887
DI ETÀ 31 ANNI
EDOARDO LEAR

The grave of Foss, in the garden of the Villa Tennyson. Foss in reality was not more than seventeen years old.

Original wash drawing to
Tennyson's 'The Miller's Daughter':
'The white chalk quarry from the
hill gleamed'. The scene is Arundel,
*c.* 1880.

He is really sadly aged and feeble – very crippled at times with rheumatism –
totters about within the house – hardly goes out at all even on his terrace just outside
the windows – has to be dressed and undressed by his manservant Luigi – and goes
to bed by 6 o'clock. . . . He still occupies himself mainly with his series of illustrations
of your father's poems – always trying some new scheme for getting them properly
reproduced in autotype with a view to publication. I am afraid it will turn out an
expensive hobby to him, even if it is successfully done. . . .

Lear decided to cut down the number of illustrations to one hundred; chopped and changed again, becoming ever more pernickety,
and, one imagines, anxious about expense; even after all schemes had
been mooted, he could not come to an arrangement with Underhill
from which he anticipated any satisfaction. He wrote to Fortescue:
'I do not work, having nothing to work on, for the great 200 A.T.
illustrations have come to grief.' The only result of all these projects,
pitiable compared with the high hopes Lear had entertained, was that
after his death a small volume was published in a limited edition,
containing three Tennyson poems (including his poem to Lear
already quoted) and twenty-two of Lear's illustrations, reduced to
exiguous proportions, with an article about Lear by Lushington.
Tennyson, rather reluctantly it seems, agreed to put his signature
to the copies, which have now become extremely rare and precious.

*Opposite below:* Lear's grave and a
memorial stone to Giorgio and his
eldest son Nicola, San Remo
cemetery.

'On the whole I do not know if I am living or dead at times,' Lear had written to Fortescue just over a year before the end. Even at this all but last moment, he could add about the friend from whose lack of sympathy and response he had suffered so much, 'I miss Lushington extremely.' His health, briefly, improved, and he went up to Biella in Piedmont for two months in the summer. The improvement did not last, and when he got back to the Villa Tennyson his memory began to fail, and during the winter he finally took to his bed. Before he died, he asked his manservant to tell Lushington, Fortescue and Northbrook that his last thoughts were of them. 'I cannot find words sufficient to thank my good friends for the good they have always done me.' His peaceful death took place on 29 January 1888, in his seventy-sixth year.

He had written the poem which is his true epitaph some years before, at the instigation of a Miss Bevan who had come to stay in San Remo, and who quoted to him something a friend had said to her: 'How pleasant to know Mr Lear!' Lear sat down and wrote a poem as playful and witty and skilful as anything he had ever written:

*Above:* The last photograph of Lear, taken in 1887.

'How pleasant to know Mr Lear!'
   Who has written such volumes of stuff:
Some think him ill-tempered and queer,
   But a few think him pleasant enough.

His mind is concrete and fastidious,
   His nose is remarkably big;
His visage is more or less hideous,
   His beard it resembles a wig.

He has ears, and two eyes, and ten fingers,
   Leastways if you reckon two thumbs;
Long ago he was one of the singers,
   But now he is one of the dumbs.

He sits in a beautiful parlour,
   With hundreds of books on the wall,
He drinks a great deal of Marsala,
   But never gets tipsy at all.

He has many friends, laymen and clerical,
   Old Foss is the name of his cat;
His body is perfectly spherical,
   He weareth a runcible hat.

When he walks in a waterproof white,
   The children run after him so!
Calling out, 'He's come out in his night-
   Gown, that crazy old Englishman, oh!'

He weeps by the side of the ocean,
   He weeps on the top of the hill;
He purchases pancakes and lotion,
   And chocolate shrimps from the mill.

He reads but he cannot speak Spanish,
   He cannot abide ginger-beer:
Ere the days of his pilgrimage vanish,
   How pleasant to know Mr Lear!

Part of a letter to Hallam Tennyson
from Franklin Lushington giving an
account of Lear's death, 29 January
1888.

Sunday Jan 29/88

My dear Hallam,

My dear dear old Lear died at
San remo today, as I hear by telegram from
Dr Hassall. He had been gradually growing
weaker all the winter – failing in memory, and
more and more disinclined to any exertion – for
some weeks entirely on his bed – occasionally
suffering much from rheumatism asthma –

His life has been dreary enough of late, tho'
in actual domestic comfort I hope he has
been as well off as he could in respect of his
servants – I was not surprised, for I have
long known from his doctor that his life was

# ACKNOWLEDGMENTS AND SELECT BIBLIOGRAPHY

The pioneer work in Lear studies is Angus Davidson's *Edward Lear: Landscape Painter and Nonsense Poet*, originally published in 1938 (London and New York) and reprinted in 1968, and as a Penguin in 1950. I acknowledge a great debt to this brilliant and moving study, and also to Vivien Noakes's *Edward Lear: The Life of a Wanderer* (London, 1968 and Boston, Mass., 1969), above all for its exceptionally detailed documentation and skilful use of the Lear archive in the Houghton Library at Harvard. There is also a useful and sympathetic brief study, *Edward Lear*, by Joanna Richardson, in the 'Writers and their Work' series (Longman's and British Council, 1965). Philip Hofer's *Edward Lear as Landscape Draughtsman* (London and Cambridge, Mass., 1968) is of prime importance in its particular field. *The Complete Nonsense of Edward Lear*, edited by Holbrook Jackson (London, 1947), reprinted many times, is the standard edition of the limericks, songs, botany, cookery and alphabets with Lear's original drawings; though important additions were made to the canon by *Teapots and Quails*, edited by Angus Davidson and Philip Hofer (London and Cambridge, Mass., 1953), and *Lear in the Original* (London and New York, 1975), the latter particularly for reproductions of Lear's original sketches to go with the limericks and of illustrations to verses other than his own. All Lear's Journals which appeared during his lifetime (see Chronology) are available in modern editions published by William Kimber (London) between 1964 and 1966, while his *Indian Journal* has been edited from the MSS by Ray Murphy (London and New York, 1953). None of his other extensive travel writings has as yet been published, nor his diaries, all of which are in the Houghton Library. In 1907 Lady Strachey edited *Letters of Edward Lear*, and followed it in 1911 with *Later Letters*, with a preface by Hubert Congreve. The majority of these letters were addressed to Chichester Fortescue (Lord Carlingford) and Lady Waldegrave. No other groups of letters, many of which still exist in private collections, have been published, nor the transcripts of his letters to his sister Ann, also preserved in the Houghton Library. Holman Hunt's reminiscences of Lear appeared in his *Pre-Raphaelitism and the Pre-Raphaelite Brotherhood* (1905). I am particularly indebted to Dr Francis Walton, of the Gennadius

Library in Athens, for his courtesy and assistance to me in my study of the valuable collection of Lear's watercolours under his care, an illustrated catalogue of which was published for a touring exhibition under the title of *Edward Lear in Greece*. I must also thank Sir Osbert Lancaster for allowing me to quote from his introduction to the catalogue of the British Council's Lear exhibition.

# CHRONOLOGY

1812 Birth at Bowman's Lodge in Holloway.

1828–32 Working in London. Publication of *Illustrations of the Family of Psittacidae*.

1832–7 Mainly at Knowsley, home of the Earls of Derby.

1838–48 Living in Rome, with occasional visits to England, and travels in southern Italy.

1845 Meets Chichester Fortescue in Rome.

1846 Publication of *Illustrated Excursions in Italy*. Gives drawing lessons to Queen Victoria. Publication of *A Book of Nonsense*.

1848–9 Travels in Greece, Albania, Ionian Islands, Egypt, and Malta, where he meets Franklin Lushington.

1849–53 Living in England, and enrols as a student in Royal Academy Schools.

1851 Publication of *Journals of a Landscape Painter in Albania, etc.*

1852 Meets Holman Hunt. Publication of *Journals of a Landscape Painter in Southern Calabria, etc.*

1853–5 Travels in Egypt, Malta, Gibraltar, Switzerland and central Europe.

1855–8 Living in Corfu, with further travels in Greece and the Near East, including Jerusalem, Damascus and Petra.

1858–60 Mainly in Rome.

1861 Returns to Corfu, which remains his base, between expeditions, until 1864. Meets Evelyn Baring. Publication of second, enlarged edition of *A Book of Nonsense*. Death of Ann Lear (sister).

1864 Ionian Islands return to Greek suzerainty. Leaves Corfu for Athens with Baring, subsequently visits Crete.

1865–7 Various travels, including extended further visit to Egypt. Summer visits to England.

1867–70 Living in Cannes, with visit to Corsica in late spring 1868.

1869 Meets Hubert Congreve.

1870 Publication of *Journal of a Landscape Painter in Corsica*.

1871 Publication of *Nonsense Songs, Stories, Botany, and Alphabets*. Moves into Villa Emily at San Remo, his home until 1881.

1872 Publication of *More Nonsense, Pictures, Rhymes, Botany, etc.* Sets out for India, but only gets as far as Suez.

1873–5 Tour of India and Ceylon.

1877 Publication of *Laughable Lyrics*.

1881 Moves out of Villa Emily and into Villa Tennyson, San Remo, his home until death. Summers spent at Monte Generoso and elsewhere above San Remo.

1883 Death of Giorgio Kokali, his manservant since 1856.

1887 Death of his cat Foss, aged seventeen.

1888 Death in January.

# LIST OF ILLUSTRATIONS

The Ganges at Benares, *c.* 1873. Watercolour by Edward Lear. Private Collection.

23 Monte Generoso, 14 August 1879. Drawing by Edward Lear. The Houghton Library, Harvard University.

24 Edward Lear with Chichester Fortescue, September 1857. Daguerreotype. By kind permission of Lord O'Hagan.

Frances, Countess Waldegrave, aged twenty-nine. Coloured lithograph after J. K. Swinton. By courtesy of the Earl Waldegrave.

25 Edward Lear, 1840. Portrait drawing by W. N. Marstrand. National Portrait Gallery, London.

26 Chichester Fortescue. Caricature by Ape. From *Vanity Fair Album*, Vol. I, 1869.

27 Franklin Lushington. Drawing by an unknown artist. Private Collection.

28 Tennyson's house at Farringford on the Isle of Wight, 1864. Drawing by Edward Lear. Tennyson Research Centre, Lincoln, published by kind permission of Lord Tennyson and the Lincolnshire Library Service.

29 Alfred and Emily Tennyson walking in the garden at Farringford with their sons Hallam and Lionel, *c.* 1862. Photograph by Rejlander. Tennyson Research Centre, Lincoln, published by kind permission of Lord Tennyson and the Lincolnshire Library Service.

30 Letter with sketch from Edward Lear to Evelyn Baring, *c.* 1862–3.

National Portrait Gallery, London.

31 Evelyn Baring, first Earl of Cromer, Photo Radio Times Hulton Picture Library.

32 Giorgio Cocali in 1881. From *Later Letters of Edward Lear to Chichester Fortescue, Frances, Countess Waldegrave and Others*, edited by Lady Strachey, 1911.

33 Petra, 1858. Watercolour by Edward Lear. Anonymous Collection

35 View of Mount Athos from near Leochorio, 21 September 1856. Pen and wash drawing by Edward Lear. Private Collection. Photo Tom Scott.

36/37 Letter with sketch of the picture gallery of his friends over his fireplace from Edward Lear to Hallam Tennyson, 30 May 1887. Tennyson Research Centre, Lincoln, published by kind permission of Lord Tennyson and the Lincolnshire Library Service.

38 Letter from Edward Lear to Emily Tennyson from Clive Vale farm, 12 October 1852. Tennyson Research Centre, Lincoln, published by kind permission of Lord Tennyson and the Lincolnshire Library Service.

39 *Our English Coasts*, 1852. Oil painting by William Holman Hunt. Tate Gallery, London.

40 William Holman Hunt, 1864. Photograph by Julia Margaret Cameron. National Portrait Gallery, London.

The Quarries of Syracuse, 12 June 1847. Pen and watercolour sketch by Edward Lear. The Walker Art Gallery, Liverpool.

41 The Quarries of Syracuse, *c.* 1850. Oil painting by Edward Lear. Photo by courtesy of Christie, Manson and Woods Ltd.

42 Sketch of Seaford. From a letter written by Edward Lear while staying at Clive Vale farm. Tennyson Research Centre, Lincoln, published by kind permission of Lord Tennyson and the Lincolnshire Library Service.

43 Sketch of Edward Lear seated at the piano. Self-caricature in pen and ink. From a letter to Evelyn Baring. Private Collection.

44 'Lear sets out from the House of Captn. Hornby, R.N.' Drawing by Edward Lear from a series of eight. Reprinted from *Lear in the Original*, 1975, with the permission of Mr H. P. Kraus.

Sketch of Edward Lear at the Royal Academy School with a skeleton leaning over him. From a letter written to Chichester Fortescue, 20 January 1850. From *Letters of Edward Lear to Chichester Fortescue and Frances, Countess Waldegrave*, edited by Lady Strachey, 1907.

45 Sketch about the painting of Masada on the Dead Sea. From a letter written by Edward Lear to Emily Tennyson, 14 June 1861. Tennyson Research Centre, Lincoln, published by kind permission of Lord Tennyson and the Lincolnshire Library Service.

46 Title-page engraving and rhyme from *A Book of Nonsense*, 1846

47 Sketch of Lear revealing his identity in a railway carriage. From a letter written by Edward Lear to Lady Waldegrave, 17 October 1866. From *Later Letters*

87 Near Calvi, 30 May 1868. Pen and watercolour by Edward Lear. Tate Gallery, London.

88–89 Sparta, 23 March 1849. Pen and watercolour by Edward Lear. Gennadius Library, Athens.

90 The Pyramids with the Sphinx and palms, 21 March 1858. Pen and watercolour by Edward Lear. Tate Gallery, London.

91 Suli, 6 May 1849. Pen and watercolour by Edward Lear. Private Collection. Photo Tom Scott.

92 Detail from a view of Parnassus, 12 April 1849. Pen and watercolour by Edward Lear. Gennadius Library, Athens.

93 Detail of the Temple of Apollo at Bassae. Oil painting by Edward Lear. Reproduced by permission of the Syndics of the Fitzwilliam Museum, Cambridge.

94 Lefkhimni, 10 May 1862. Pen and watercolour by Edward Lear. Private Collection. Photo Tom Scott.

Potamos, 8 and 23 April 1862 and 28 January 1864. Pen and watercolour by Edward Lear. Private Collection. Photo Tom Scott.

95 Corfu, 21 April 1866. Pen and watercolour by Edward Lear. Gennadius Library, Athens.

96 Athens, 8 April 1849. Pen and watercolour by Edward Lear. Gennadius Library, Athens.

97 Mycenae, 31 March 1849. Pen and watercolour by Edward Lear. Gennadius Library, Athens.

98 Delphi, 16 April 1849. Pen and watercolour by Edward Lear. Gennadius Library, Athens.

99 Suda Bay, 24 May 1864. Pen and watercolour by Edward Lear. Gennadius Library, Athens.

Aptera, Crete, 4 May 1864. Pen and watercolour by Edward Lear. Gennadius Library, Athens.

100 Villa Emily as it is today. Photo by courtesy of Roger Musgrave.

Lear with Foss the cat. Sketch from a letter written by Edward Lear to Emily Tennyson, 5 January 1876. Tennyson Research Centre, Lincoln, published by kind permission of Lord Tennyson and the Lincolnshire Library Service.

101 Group photograph showing Lord Northbrook, Viceroy of India, and Evelyn Baring, c. 1873. Photo Radio Times Hulton Picture Library.

102 Roorkee, 20 March 1874. Pen and watercolour by Edward Lear. The Houghton Library, Harvard University.

103 Agra, the Taj Mahal, 1874. Pen and watercolour by Edward Lear. The Houghton Library, Harvard University.

104 Giorgio and Lear on an elephant. Sketch from a letter written by Edward Lear to Lady Waldegrave, 25 October 1875. Somerset Record Office, Taunton, by kind permission of Lord O'Hagan.

Poona, 1874. Watercolour by Edward Lear. The Houghton Library, Harvard University.

105 Kinchinjunga, near Darjeeling, 1873–4. Oil painting by Edward Lear. Private Collection.

106 Letter from Edward Lear to Emily Tennyson, 18 August 1883. Tennyson Research Centre, Lincoln, published by kind permission of Lord Tennyson and the Lincolnshire Library Service.

107 Photograph of Emily Tennyson. Tennyson Research Centre, Lincoln, published by kind permission of Lord Tennyson and the Lincolnshire Library Service.

108 The hotel that blocked Lear's view from the Villa Emily, as it is today. Photo by courtesy of Roger Musgrave.

109 Letter from Edward Lear to Hallam Tennyson, 16 September 1880. Tennyson Research Centre, Lincoln, published by kind permission of Lord Tennyson and the Lincolnshire Library Service.

110 The Villa Tennyson under construction. Sepia photograph. Photo by courtesy of Roger Musgrave.

111 The Villa Tennyson completed. Sepia photograph. Photo by courtesy of Roger Musgrave.

112 Lear and Foss. Sketch from a letter written by Edward Lear to Hallam Tennyson, 16 June 1884. Tennyson Research Centre, Lincoln, published by kind permission of Lord Tennyson and the Lincolnshire Library Service.

113 The grave of Foss in the garden of the Villa Tennyson. From *Later Letters of Edward Lear to Chichester Fortescue, Frances, Countess Waldegrave and Others*, edited by Lady Strachey, 1911.

114 Scene in Arundel, England, c. 1880. Original wash drawing by

Edward Lear to Tennyson's poem *The Miller's Daughter*. Tennyson Research Centre, Lincoln, published by kind permission of Lord Tennyson and the Lincolnshire Library Service.

115 The last photograph of Lear, taken in 1887. Photo Radio Times Hulton Picture Library.

The graves of Lear and Nicola Cocali in San Remo cemetery. Photo by courtesy of Roger Musgrave.

116 Two self-caricatures. From a letter written by Edward Lear to Alfred Tennyson, 27 June 1864. Tennyson Research Centre, Lincoln, published by kind permission of Lord Tennyson and the Lincolnshire Library Service.

117 Part of a letter from Franklin Lushington to Hallam Tennyson giving an account of Edward Lear's death, 29 January 1888. Tennyson Research Centre, Lincoln, published by

kind permission of Lord Tennyson and the Lincolnshire Library Service.

124 Monte Generoso, 5 August 1878. Pen and watercolour by Edward Lear. Private Collection. Photo courtesy of Sotheby Co.

128 Lear with two garden snails. Sketch from a letter written by Edward Lear possibly to Augusta Bethell, *c.* 1881. Photo by courtesy of Roger Musgrave.

Monte Generoso, pen and watercolour, 4.00–5.30 p.m., 5 August 1878.

# INDEX

*Page numbers in italics refer to illustrations*

The last page of a letter by Lear possibly written to Augusta Bethell, *c.* 1881: 'My garden is now admirably beautiful, and were it not for the slugs and snails would be inimitable. But those melancholy mucilaginous molluscs have eaten up all my Higher‑cynths and also my Lower‑cynths, and I have only just found a mode of getting rid of these enemies; – which is by flattering their vanity in taking them friendly walks up and down the garden, – an inganno [trick] which blinds them to ulterior consequences. And thus, (they being of a monstrous size as you may see by the sketches below,) when I get them near the cistern, I pitch them into the water, where they justly expiate their unpleasant and greedy sins.'